BRIDGING THE GAP

A Training Module in Personal and Professional Development

Judy Hildebrand

Foreword by
Gill Gorell Barnes

Systemic Thinking and Practice Series

Series Editors
David Campbell & Ros Draper

London
KARNAC BOOKS

First published in 1998 by
H. Karnac (Books) Ltd.
58 Gloucester Road
London SW7 4QY

Copyright © 1998 Judy Hildebrand
Foreword copyright © 1998 Gill Gorell Barnes
Chapter 8 copyright © 1998 Colette Richardson & Frankie Zimmerman

Illustrations by Jo Nesbitt, Amsterdam, The Netherlands

British Library Cataloguing in Publication Data

A C.I.P. record for this book is available from the British Library.

ISBN 1 85575 181 X

Edited, designed, and produced by Communication Crafts

Printed in Great Britain by BPC Wheatons Ltd, Exeter

10 9 8 7 6 5 4 3 2 1

CONTENTS

ACKNOWLEDGEMENTS

I would like to thank all my colleagues at the Tavistock Clinic and the Institute of Family Therapy who provided the opportunity and support necessary to develop the personal and professional development (PPD) modules in both centres.

The original idea for the PPD modules stemmed from discussions between myself and my colleague Dr. Arnon Bentovim. We had previously worked together as co-therapists and as group leaders and were actively involved in the training of family therapists. I would like to acknowledge the importance of his contribution both in the development of the PPD concept and in his role as co-leader of the large group, as discussed in Chapter 3.

I am indebted to Colette Richardson and Frankie Zimmerman for undertaking the unique trainee survey described in Chapter 8 and for all their hard work, enthusiasm, and ideas.

A special thank you not only to the trainees who gave their time to participate in the consumer survey but also to all those trainees who have taken part in a module and thereby helped to fashion it.

I am grateful to Bebe Speed for her invaluable comments which were both constructive and encouraging at the draft stage. Thanks also to Brenda Cox from The Family Institute in Cardiff and Barbara Warner from the Prudence Skynner Unit in London for sharing their ideas about trainees' personal and professional development during training.

Finally, I would like to thank Helene Curtis for her continuing support and encouragement.

EDITORS' FOREWORD

For some, the dust is settling over the development of family therapy technique, and therapists are re-discovering the basic processes that make therapy work. For example, there is increasing interest in the nature of the therapeutic relationship and the use of the self in family therapy, and this is reflected in training courses that emphasize the personal growth and awareness of the therapist. Judy Hildebrand is known throughout the family therapy field as someone who has always spoken for integrating formal aspects of therapy training with personal development, and she has designed and run such workshops for courses in Britain and Europe for many years.

The book presents a thorough discussion of the thorny issues about what makes a good therapist. Is personal development different from therapy? Should therapists in training have personal therapy? If so, should their own families be involved in some way? What is the most appropriate way to build personal development into the structure of a training course?

The heart of the book consists of the exercises that Hildebrand has used in her workshops over many years. They have been refined and honed, like polished gemstones, through the trial-and-error process that can only be sustained by a very experienced trainer, and they are presented in an accessible form that clarifies how to run the exercises and what pitfalls to avoid. Some exercises are about families of origin and their relation to our "trigger" families, and others focus on the way we develop our own style and techniques. But the picture would be incomplete without understanding the effect that the exercises have on personal development, and for this volume she is joined by Collette Richardson and Frankie Zimmerman, two colleagues and ex-trainees, who have collated the experiences of a range of trainees from the courses and are able to complement Hildebrand's ideas with the voice of the trainee.

The book opens a very important debate for the family therapy field. At a time of treatment rationing and standard setting, it aptly draws our attention to an issue of increasing importance: training the highest-quality family therapists. In addition, it offers trainers and supervisors an invaluable "how-to-do-it" guide to tried-and-tested methods of taking trainees through a programme of personal and professional development.

David Campbell
Ros Draper
London
March 1998

FOREWORD

Gill Gorell Barnes

F amily therapy training in Britain has now been established for over twenty years, yet many issues about the requirements of training within the field remain unresolved. One of the missing agreed ingredients in the variations of the training recipe has been the "person of the therapist" and the therapists' use of self within the work that they do. Is "the use of self" important, and how is "self" to be defined within a framework that sometimes argues for a multiplicity of contextually defined selves rather than a "core" self? Put a slightly different way, how are training courses to develop the appropriate complexity within trainees' thinking and responsivity to equip them for the variety of complex interpersonal encounters their work is likely to entail? A major stumbling block in training has been to find a model for attending to such questions which offers overall congruence to a systemic approach to work with relational systems, rather than relying on a model of individual "therapy for the therapist" seen to devolve from an intra-psychically oriented model.

The United Kingdom Council for Psychotherapy and the recent introduction of a European Certificate in Psychotherapy have each made it a requirement for qualified practitioners in all forms of psychotherapy to have done "personal work " for some hundreds of hours as part of their qualifying training. While many therapeutic trainings have not seen psychotherapy based on a psychoanalytic model as suiting their own form of training, and many have substituted the experience of the kind of therapy that they are teaching as part of what the trainee must undergo subjectively, family therapy and systemic training has never decided that therapy for therapists within the context of their own family should be a part of the training of all family therapists. Some courses have had discussions about "bringing the family of the trainee in" as part of the training experience, but this has never, to my knowledge, been mandatory and, indeed, might be seen by many families as an infringement of civil liberties. If work on the "self", however defined, is to be a training requirement with sufficient depth and meaning, how then is it to be done?

Judy Hildebrand, in her long experience as a clinical trainer and supervisor, has gone some way towards addressing this gap in the field, through the work she has developed with trainees over the last ten years. Taking as her starting point the need to devise ways of looking at the self which reflect some of the immediacy and complexity of the experience of family therapy, in which transformation of experience can take place from a number of different positions simultaneously, she has worked with students using experiential and reflective tasks that promote greater self-reflexivity, lead to an increased perception of the complexity of the process of change in oneself and in others, and make a difference to competence in practice. While she does not claim that the personal and professional module she describes is an alternative to personal therapy, she suggests that as a path in its own right it offers a way for each systemic therapist in training to develop some of the necessary edges of experience for considering the reverberations between self and other in the arena of the therapeutic interview.

The module she describes also reflects some other aspects of the systemic approach. Work takes place in public, within the context defined by the course, the boundary being held by all the participants, including the module leader. Trainees are therefore encouraged to voice aspects of their personal experience in ways that parallel the experience they will be asking of family members.

Action, reflection, and narrative about personal experience form part of the learning about "self in context". Experience is shared with others in a process of mutual learning and teaching. In working with others while working on the self, trainees are offered an experience of shared emotional and cognitive change which characterizes much of what may take place in a family session.

This book is therefore very welcome, not only in its own right as a contribution towards the development of therapeutic complexity in systemic training, but also as a contribution towards the ongoing debate about what constitutes systemic therapy and the role of the therapist.

INTRODUCTION

For many years, the complex topic of how best to train family therapists, in terms of integrating their personal experience and their professional learning, has remained controversial; many family therapy trainers are concerned about trainees not having an acknowledged method of self-preparation consistent with a systemic model. Different institutions have different requirements and use different training methods consistent with their specific systemic theoretical model. In America, different states impose differing professional requirements whereas in Europe there is neither consensus nor a universal mandatory policy requiring trainees to have undergone some form of psychotherapy, be it in terms of the individual, the couple, or the family (Onnis, 1997). Nonetheless, in practice a large number of family therapy trainees have had some prior experience of therapy or personal work, usually in a one-to-one context. Personal psychoanalytically based individual therapy, whilst potentially helpful to the individual, in the systemic context provides a self-contradictory proposition.

One result of attempts to further our thinking and practice about this issue has been the personal and professional development (PPD) module, currently being used on MSc courses in family therapy at two different institutions. The module is a compulsory, though non-assessed, component of the training and continues throughout the two years' duration of the courses.

The module aims to provide a lively forum in which personal and professional interactions are discussed, where experiential exercises are used to link past and present, where group dynamics and course issues are recognized, and where linked skills training is practised.

In this group-based structure, the focus is on the connections between the personal and the professional experience of the trainee and how these can be used to develop professional expertise and self-reflexivity (the latter concept is discussed in Chapter 2). In the PPD module, a heuristic approach is adopted such that trainees have to take responsibility for what they learn and what they integrate in other aspects of the course. This module is predicated on the assumption, yet to be adequately researched, that the trainee's wider awareness of "self in context" leads to improved professional practice and is therefore to the benefit of both the client and the therapist. Characteristic of this form of groupwork are the feedback loops between personal and professional issues and between them and wider systems such as the extended family, economic, social, and political structures.

The opening chapters are concerned with the context and evolution of the PPD module meetings. Chapter 1 describes the background, the aims, and the rationale that have led to the establishment of the PPD module currently in use in two postgraduate family therapy trainings. Chapter 2 focuses on current professional concerns about the significance of trainees becoming more self-reflexive and the role of personal therapy in family therapy training. Chapter 3 then describes the structure of the PPD module in two institutions using the model.

Chapter 4 looks at the module content, with particular emphasis on the experiential exercises, each of which is described, together with additional comments and caveats, in step-by-step stages in Chapters 5, 6, and 7.

Chapter 8 presents responses to interviews with a number of family therapy trainees who had been participants in the PPD modules in two different institutions from 1993 to 1995. Based on their analysis of this survey, the two interviewers (Colette Richardson and Frankie Zimmerman) consider possible improvements in the design of the module.

Chapter 9 opens a discussion of the various themes raised throughout the book and considers implications for future training.

Author's note

For the purposes of clarity, therapists and leaders are referred to as female and trainees as male. "Group leader" refers to the author unless otherwise stated.

BRIDGING THE GAP

CHAPTER ONE

Aims and rationale

In the early stages of its development, one way of distinguishing family therapy theory and practice from other psychotherapies was by the lack of focus on the person of the systemic therapist. However, given that family therapy has now become an established therapeutic modality and a profession in its own right, this urge to be so strongly differentiated in this respect may no longer be so pressing. I would suggest that the time has come to reappraise the role of self and its significance in clinical practice.

Over the years I had become increasingly aware of the division drawn between personal and professional dimensions of training, as if they were not mutually influential. In addition, whilst I felt confident about the quality of academic achievement on training courses, I was less sanguine about the overall level of clinical expertise. In my view, therapists needed a more sophisticated degree of self-knowledge not only to differentiate between their clients' and their own attributions and belief systems, but also in order to become more sensitive to the experience of being in therapy.

. . . I want to engage the family in an interactive process that leads to an experiential exchange. In order for the process of therapy to be impactful rather than merely educational or social, it must consist of real experiences, not just head trips. [Whitaker & Bumberry, 1988, p. 56]

I share Haber's (1990) view that

. . . asking trainees to share their personal histories creates a fine boundary between therapy and training. However, it offers trainees an opportunity to evolve individually, interpersonally, and professionally. Most importantly, working with personal rules and myths derived from one's family of origin could offer a shortcut to dealing with professional handicaps.

A model of personal work therefore seemed an essential component in the movement from academic learning to clinical practice. However, it had become evident from contact with many trainees over the years that some had little or no previous experience of personal, couple, or family therapy.

In their survey on stress and the practice of family therapy, Street and Rivett (1996) asked family therapists to indicate their experience of personal therapy: 54% reported that they had undergone individual therapy and 24.7% marital therapy, compared to only 9.4% who had undergone family therapy. Interestingly, many of those who had had experience of family therapy had also experienced marital or individual therapy. The authors expressed the view that since

. . . few family therapists have experienced marital or family therapy as consumers . . . [t]hey may consequently fail to appreciate their clients' perspective. . . . Since personal therapy appears to reduce stress by increasing personal resources, trainers should consider including an element of therapy in training courses. [p. 317]

At the Association of Family Therapy conference in 1994, an audience of approximately 150 family therapists was asked how many of them had been in therapy; in response, more than three-quarters indicated that they had. When asked how many of them had been in individual therapy, the vast majority kept their hands up; when asked how many had been in couple therapy, approximately 10 indicated that they had. However, when asked how many people had opted for family therapy, only 5 people put their hands up, and they were nearly all Dutch!

Stemming from the early discussions with Arnon Bentovim, I had hypothesized that personal therapy—that is, a structured opportunity for self-reflexivity—would lead to better-prepared and possibly less biased and more understanding therapists. Clearly, we had been influenced by our personal experiences of being in individual therapy; both of us had been in psychoanalytically based therapies and had recognized the relevance of the process in linking our personal and professional lives. I still wonder what I may have missed by not having a personal experience of family therapy. However, not all family therapists agree with the premise that personal therapy necessarily improves the quality of clinical practice. Haley (1996), discussing whether or not personal therapy makes for a better therapist, states that where trainees' biases cause problems in therapy, that should be dealt with by the supervisor and that personal therapy is not the solution.

In practice, however, in supervision there is little time to pursue all the issues that arise. Furthermore, trainees may feel inhibited about exposing themselves too much in supervision, because it is an assessed component of their training. "People cannot reconsider their prejudices when they feel under threat" (Cecchin, Lane, & Ray, 1994, p. 30).

Another important influence on our thinking was the way in which we ourselves had trained as family therapists. In the mid-1970s, when I was first involved, family therapy was at the toddler stage in this country, and, in company with colleagues, we all had to learn by experimentation. Aside from reading the literature, which was predominantly American, we engaged in workshops, drawing genograms, sculpting, trying out new techniques, discussing new ideas, and sharing life stories. Inevitably this was an active phase in our learning, and, for many of us, that lively process continued to have a significant effect on the way we taught and trained subsequent generations of therapists. Having been stimulated and enthused by the various active methods of learning more about my own experiences of being a family member, I wanted to provide a similar opportunity for others.

I was fortified and strongly influenced by Whitaker's view

> . . . that we must all reinvent the wheel in order to be therapists. We must grapple with life and ourselves until we can see beneath the surface. We must have some connection with and access to our own impulses, intuitions and associations. Only when you've struggled with yourself are you free to bring your person, not just your therapist's uniform, into the therapy room. [Whitaker & Bumberry, 1988, p. 40]

As a result, rather than waiting for consensus between family therapy trainers about a policy regarding therapy, we took the decision to begin some personal work in a new module focusing on linking the past to the present, the personal to the professional. As if to emphasize the latter, the module also included experimentation with a range of alternative interventions to deal with clinical difficulties that the trainees encountered in their practice.

By designing the original module to encourage more personal exploration, Bentovim and I were demonstrating our view that this issue should be more actively addressed and incorporated in the training of family therapists. However, we were under no illusion that the module could either replace or provide the same resource as personal therapy. We hoped to focus on the effects of personal experience on professional practice rather than on a consideration of the significance and meaning of each trainee's personal experience. The point was whether the module could provide a rich source of learning and experimentation even in cases where a trainee had prior experience of personal, couple, or family therapy. Despite the fact that the majority of senior family therapy trainers and many trainees have some experience of personal therapy, there is still a lack of consensus about whether therapy should be a requirement prior to or during training and, if so, what form this should take. As Cooklin (1994) comments, "the exact paths whereby therapists are to expand their repertoire, overcome blocks, or discover and utilise hidden resources . . . is usually not spelt out" (p. 287).

CHAPTER TWO

The use of self-reflexivity in family therapy training

T he focus of this discussion is based on the view

. . . that family therapy has reached a cross-roads in respect of its attention to the exploration of 'self'—in
therapy and thus in training. . . . It is imperative that the personal is addressed . . . in order to successfully complete a training, a trainee must be able to recognise and understand patterns
from within their own significant relationship systems (past and
present) and culture which may help and/or hinder their work.
[Mason, 1997]

Despite the fact that many British family therapy training institutions have considered previous personal therapy an advantage,
there have been no concerted moves towards integrating this in
a systemic framework and making the experience a condition of
training. Although they share an overarching systemic theory, different schools of family therapy have, over time and to varying
degrees, addressed or by-passed the issue of the person of the
therapist and her use of self. The major stumbling block appears to
be finding a way to attend to the issue that would be generalizable
to all models within the systemic framework. Significant influences

for change have included the major shift in the theoretical position of the post-Milan group when the therapist was recognized as part of the system. This resulted in a reappraisal of the use of self, of the therapist's own values, and of the need to incorporate these aspects in theory and practice.

Another influence was the development of the constructionist orientation to family therapy, which promoted a reconceptualization of the therapeutic use of self (Real, 1990). Following this, Aponte (1994) introduced his innovative person/practice model of training based on the premise that therapy challenges clinicians to use

> . . . their personal selves effectively within the professional relationship. The personal component of this relationship is not about some general liking and acceptance of clients. It is specific to the goals and means of therapy. Thus therapists need training that both opens them to themselves and teaches them vulnerability, discipline, and freedom within the relationship. [p. 3]

In discussing this topic I have chosen to use the term self-reflexivity, with its connotation of a more systemic stance, to differentiate it from the concept of self-awareness; the latter is reminiscent of a person-centred, objective "truth-seeking" position as described by Hedges and Lang (1993). They also clearly delineate the similarities, differences, aims, and intended outcomes of self-reflexivity and self-awareness (p. 285). I agree with Boscolo and Bertrando (1996) that "Both the therapist's and the client's inner and external worlds and the relationship with the social systems in which they are embedded have become the territory to be explored. Self-reflexivity has taken clearly a central position" (p. 14).

Taking a historical perspective, Hedges and Lang (1993) comment on trainers who in the 1970s and early 1980s reported moving from a psychodynamically influenced programme using experiential groups focusing on personal work, towards a preference for the teaching of skills, using video and live supervision. Where the focus has been on the person of the therapist (Aponte, 1994; Aponte & Winter, 1992; Bowen, 1978), the emphasis has predominantly been on training needs, such as the therapist recognizing trigger issues that might affect her clinical practice. This has commonly been addressed on the basis of genogram work (Francis, 1988;

Hardy & Laszloffy, 1995) or in relation to sculpting (Duhl, Kantor, & Duhl, 1973; Heinl, 1987). The use of genograms and of mapping (Hedges & Lang, 1993) and the development of the self of the therapist (McDaniel & Landau-Stanton, 1991, p. 470) are well-known and valued approaches. Hopefully the more recent focus on the significance of the self of the therapist (Cooklin, 1994; Haber, 1994) signals a return to even more emphasis on the essential interplay between professional acumen and personal development, emphasising the artificiality of considering them as distinct entities. There have been other influences in this direction, too—particularly the current interest in the therapeutic use of narrative, which has played a part in reawakening interest in the significance of the trainees' personal stories. The importance of recognizing the significance of trainees' own life experience is commented on by Lindsey (1993):

> Their (the trainees') personal life script contributes to how they interpret the family's stories, the meaning of therapy and the therapeutic relationship. This in turn is contextualised by the beliefs and experiences in the families they have grown up in and in the families they have created—the personal life script is affected by the norms of the community of which the therapist is a part and which may powerfully influence the values held about family life. [p. 307]

Flaskas and Perlesz (1996) also point out that

> Therapists are increasingly being invited by their supervisors, their peer teams, and their own sense of professional responsibility to scrutinise the contribution made to the progress of stuckness of therapy by their own inner life, families of origin, current life circumstances, "prejudices," or culture, gender, and ethnicity. [p. 220]

It may be that as family therapy is now a respected and established form of psychotherapy, we can afford to take some further risks and look more critically at the quality of our clinical practice, its connection with the self-reflexivity of the therapist and the ways in which we prepare the next generation of therapists and trainers.

Burck (1995) comments on developments in the family therapy field over the previous five years, with reference to the training of therapists and the use of self:

In the training of family therapists, . . . ideas of the importance of the therapist's contribution to what is observed and discussed in therapy, has led to a much greater emphasis on therapists' personal/professional development and their use of self in therapy. Managing the tensions of being a "participant/observer," both a participant/observer in the therapy, embedded in it, yet attempting to develop and maintain "self-reflexivity," are now crucial aspects of the training. [p. 249]

Blow and Piercy (1997) believe that to fulfil our responsibility for producing the most effective therapists possible, a significant portion of training should be in developing personal agency—that is, the ability and freedom to access personal resources. In their view, such training should be presented as a core element across theories and should be overt, focused, and experiential.

Even if the various schools of family therapy were to agree in principle that personal therapy was an appropriate and desirable context for promoting both self-reflexivity and a more sophisticated use of self in therapy with clients, we would still be faced with the issue of a possible lack of congruence between the model of personal therapy usually undertaken—predominantly *individual*—and a systemic model based on *couple* or *family* therapy in the professional training. This is less a question of numbers and more that of the discrepant theory bases for the trainee therapist who is in personal psychoanalytic psychotherapy while training as a systemic therapist. From the reports of trainees who attempted to juggle the two theory bases at the same time, the experience was extremely confusing.

CHAPTER THREE

The structure of the personal and professional development module

I n this chapter the focus is on four main areas:

1. *The institutional contexts* in which the personal and professional development module was developed

2. *The groupwork model* on which the module was based

3. *Leadership of the module*

4. *The life-cycle of groups* within the module

THE INSTITUTIONAL CONTEXTS

Early in the 1990s, the personal and professional development (PPD) module was introduced into two major British institutions offering family therapy training at MSc level. Not surprisingly, the introduction of a new module such as the PPD created difficulties for MSc convenors already struggling with so many competing demands on course time. Nonetheless, I was given a free hand to devise the module within the time constraint, and agreement was reached about both compulsory attendance and confidentiality. In addition, it was decided to leave genogram work to be done as part of the supervision component of the MSc, so that supervisors would be able to make immediate links between their trainees' previous life experience and their clinical practice.

This book draws on my experience of leading three large groups and three small groups, each group being worked with over the two-year period of the MSc training (see Exhibit 1). There was a marked difference in the numbers of participants on the courses in the two institutions, which gave me the opportunity to compare and contrast large and small groups using a similar module.

INSTITUTION A

LARGE GROUP

36 PARTICIPANTS

2 LEADERS—MALE, FEMALE
(external to the MSc course)

The group meets once per academic term for three and a half
hours over the two years

INSTITUTION B

SMALL GROUP

9–12 PARTICIPANTS

1 LEADER—FEMALE
(who is also a supervisor, tutor,
and trainer on the MSc course)

The group meets for nine hours during the first week
of the academic term and subsequently for three hours every
three weeks over the two years

Exhibit 1

THE GROUPWORK MODEL

Group leaders have a clear remit to respond to group issues, to help trainees recognize the connections and circularity between their personal and professional functioning, and, as a result of that understanding, to develop new professional skills.

The groupwork model employed on these training courses is akin to the systemic groupwork approach as described in Burck, Hildebrand, and Mann (1996), in which group interpretations were not used and transference or countertransference issues were not directly discussed. Questions were designed to encourage an expansion of perspectives and to link with the individual's wider systems. Much of the time in the PPD module is spent in general discussion about issues brought up by the participants, as well as in doing exercises relevant to the feelings and subjects that they raise. In addition, these are linked to the exploration and practice of new techniques for use in their clinical practice. So as well as an exploration of their personal and professional connections, there are also specific training aspects. Hopefully, this format reflects hybrid vigour rather than model muddle.

Consistent with my aim to focus on the interactive processes between the personal and professional aspects of training, I deliberately keep to this task rather than seeing the module as a means of providing therapy, either for the individual or for the group as a whole. That is not to say that group dynamics or individual concerns are ignored—to the contrary—but they are dealt with in connection with the wider task. The aim is for trainees to experience the module as a forum in which they can safely raise difficult thoughts and feelings and take opportunities for making personal discoveries. However, given the irregularity and infrequency of meetings, as well as the number of participants involved in the large groups, this may not always be a realistic expectation.

Group leaders are responsible for designing the modules and setting the scene, but the content must be a collaborative effort with the trainees. I recognize that some individuals will be more comfortable than others with this open, self-reflexive method of learning in a group context. Trainees, who are used to intensive individual or group psychotherapy, in which their behaviour or attitudes may be subject to interpretation, may find this heuristic approach both unexpected and disappointing.

LEADERSHIP OF THE MODULE

Inevitably, each group leader will carry out the task according to her personal style; dependent on her systemic model, she may be more or less interventionist. Her approach to the task will also be influenced by her previous groupwork experience and the require- ment here for an active, flexible approach. The model proposed by Burck et al. (1996) fits well—that is, one in which self-disclosure by the group leader may be used both as a joining technique and as an encouragement to share personal experiences. Most importantly, as in any system, the participants' interactions with the group leader will create idiosyncratic group dynamics affecting the lead- er's approach.

> On one occasion a small group was spontaneously discussing anxieties about talking to children in therapy. After some further airing of the subject, this stimulated me to devise a new experien- tial exercise. The trainees were asked to think of themselves at a particularly young age and of someone whom they had liked talking to—and someone they did not. They were then asked to think about what did or did not make those exchanges pleasant. They then discussed this in the group. Finally, they were asked to reflect on how these past experiences could help or hinder their clinical practice. We ended with a few short role-plays to practise different responses and to complete the personal/professional links.

As a module leader, my aim is to cover the following four linked stages within each group meeting; however, the degree of empha- sis on any particular stage may vary from one meeting to another:

- *group preoccupations*
- *personal experience*
- *professional dilemmas*
- *interventions*

Sometimes, trying to cover all these areas and linking them to the group's issues within such a short period can feel like a balancing act. The art is, I think, in allowing the work to develop organically out of the group themes and atmosphere. It can be difficult: a group leader has to manage several tensions, such as between the content and the process within the group, between individual and group needs, between affect and skills learning. In addition, the significance of the trainees' life-cycle stage and status, both on the course and in the wider context of work and home life, must also be held in mind, and all these will affect the way in which the trainees choose to use the module.

Although a leader's style is bound to be idiosyncratic, it is essential to be able to engage quickly with a group of trainees and to understand the aims and the demands of their training. Over the last six years, I have worked with cohorts of trainees ranging in number from nine to thirty-six and have always found that my first task was to establish an appropriate atmosphere for the group to work in; hence, joining and engaging processes were extremely important. As a result, my style has been informal and friendly, using self-disclosure, encouraging active participation, providing containment, and acknowledging responsibility for a module in which personal matters and their impact on clinical development could be discussed in confidence. I am doubtful that a more traditional, passive groupwork model, in which the leader is listening and sometimes commenting on general themes, would achieve the level of interaction and shared experience that I aim to achieve in the time available. In the model I am proposing, group leaders are required to be directive in terms of maintaining a focus, to initiate experiential exercises, and to introduce relevant skills development. Since trainees tend to be influenced by one model more than another, it is helpful if leaders have a range of methods at their disposal so as to encourage trainees to make a more considered choice of the therapeutic interventions that they employ in their clinical work.

Co-leadership

In the original module in the large group setting (Institution A), I had assumed that Arnon Bentovim and I working as a male–female pair would find this helpful in managing gender issues in discussion and would avoid dominance by either sex. I am aware that some readers may consider this male–female approach as a reflection of a traditionalist view of a "parenting" model, which it is, but it seemed a pragmatic acknowledgement of both sexes.

Burck and Daniel (1995) make interesting comments on gender aspects in training and supervision and cite an interesting example of one way to identify and address potential dilemmas for the male–female pair at a process level. Anticipating some conflict over whether the female or her male colleague would take control of the session, Daniel asked the group at the beginning of the workshop to make a hypothesis about how they thought gender issues would be reflected in the process between the trainers, to observe the progress of their hypothesis during the course, and then to make comments. The writers subsequently noted that, "This proved to be a useful intervention to the trainers in developing reflexivity as well". This would also be a useful addition to the exercises presented in Chapters 4–7.

In my experience, working as one of a pair of leaders with large numbers of trainees felt more relaxed and provided opportunities for us to model how we dealt with uncertainties or differences during the session. Because there were two of us, we could also circulate and provide more detailed attention to smaller working units when the larger group was divided up for particular exercises. I wonder whether two leaders would feel "top-heavy" in a group of fewer than ten, where the ratio of staff to trainees would be that much higher. If the group leaders were also staff members on the course, it is less likely that the group would feel that the module was separate from the assessed parts of the course. In any case it would be less economic to employ two leaders.

In my view, co-leaders in this context need as much preparation as co-therapists. Mutual respect and confidence, as well as a shared attitude to the use of humour and spontaneity in pursuing issues, are all essential. As I mentioned previously, Bentovim and I had worked together as co-therapists and group leaders, and we both used an integrative approach. Our task was also made easier by dint of being recognized as experienced trainers, supervisors, and clinicians, who had also contributed to the literature. Perhaps the fact that despite this we were very willing to share our experiences and valued those of the participants was what really mattered. The value of sharing a theoretical base with a co-leader seems obvious; perhaps less so is the advantage of having a wide experience of having worked in different models with patient, staff, and training groups. An understanding of group dynamics, an ability to evoke and use group input creatively, thinking in terms of the individuals' wider systems, experience of leading task-oriented groups, and teaching experience all add to the richness of a leader's role and effectiveness. The PPD module offers an exciting opportunity to create an idiosyncratic systemic approach that integrates aspects of a variety of relevant groupwork models.

Leadership and multiple roles

When the PPD module was introduced in the large group context, neither group leader was involved in other roles on the MSc course. It seemed that the module group leader should ideally be someone from outside the course so as to avoid the multiplicity of hats that a course staff member would have to wear. We thought that working from within the system could lead to tensions between what might be seen as competing roles, and was also at variance with traditional groupwork practice. It seemed too complicated and unwieldy to be a tutor, a supervisor, a lecturer, and possibly a leader of the PPD module as well. There was also concern about whether the groups would trust an internal leader and would be worried that confidential information from the group context would be used when trainee assessments were made. This issue of hierarchy and power cannot be ignored, but it may be somewhat mitigated by the openness and appropriate use of relevant self-disclosure by the leader(s). However, because of the overall authority of the course organizer(s), it is not advisable to combine the roles of course organizer and PPD module leader since this might prove overwhelmingly confusing and inhibit trainees from expressing their personal uncertainties.

A more positive view is that where the module leader is also a member of staff, she would have current knowledge about the content, the structure, and periods of particular stress attached to the course and when and how this might impact on the group.

Therefore, despite considerable misgivings about the duplication of my roles, I agreed to take on the role of internal module leader with a smaller group in another institution because of my previous experience with the PPD module. One advantage was economic: an outsider would be an additional expense, whereas as a staff member I was already salaried. Another was that this could provide an opportunity to consider the viability of different-size modules and to compare and contrast the trainees' experience in the small and large groups. As commented on in Chapter 8, the advantages and disadvantages of an external versus an internal module leader remains a live issue.

As a supervisor for the course at Institution B, I had anticipated that leadership of the module might create some tension for the trainees from my own supervision group. Overall it probably did have an inhibiting effect on them and on me, particularly in the early stages of the course. During role-plays I was aware of avoiding being either too affirmative or too challenging towards my own supervisees. I also felt that when the trainees criticized aspects of the course, they were very careful not to talk in terms of specific staff members. I understood this to be an issue of respect for the staff and the awareness of potentially putting me, in role as the module leader, "on the spot", creating a possible conflict of loyalties. Additionally, at course meetings of staff and trainee representatives, there were occasions when I experienced some "restraint" by the latter when the PPD was discussed; any inclination to become protective and defensive of either the staff or the trainees can be quite powerful and is, of course, likely to be unproductive. More typically these issues were dealt with in general discussion in the module, sometimes culminating in a clarification by the trainees of how *they* intended to manage a problem. On a very few occasions, when the trainees suggested an improvement that could immediately be brought to a staff meeting, or where there were complaints about the way the staff had disseminated important information, the trainees asked the module leader to raise the issue at a staff level, but generally they preferred to deal with the staff themselves, which seemed more satisfactory.

The following is a typical example of dealing with a complaint raised in the group.

At the beginning of the second year, one group was very despondent about the thought of the onerous amount of work awaiting them. After a lengthy discussion and much complaint, I devised the following exercise:

A. The group members were asked to do the following individually and without comment:
   i. Think of what someone close to you might say and do when feeling fed up and overwhelmed.
   ii. Think about the main themes that they raise.
   iii. Consider the effect that this has on you and how you would respond.
B. The group then divided into pairs to discuss this.
C. Finally, they were asked to think about their own patterns of response to frustration and irritation.

Reconvening in the group, some trainees described their experiences with diagrams on the board, demonstrating the coping strategies that they had developed individually or with their partners. The effect of the exercise was to reduce their tension, to feel that their frustration was shared, that it related to the reality of the pressures on them, but that there were also challenges and excitement ahead. They also gleaned useful suggestions from their peers about coping mechanisms.

This led to a further discussion and two role-plays in the next meeting, in which trainees commented on the irritation and discomfort they experienced when they felt that clients in their frustration demanded answers and solutions, or when they felt under fire because the clients were angry that their difficulties had not been resolved. In the role-plays, we looked for moments of impasse, when the group could offer alternative interventions that the therapist could use. The aim was to demonstrate that there is no one "right" way of dealing with these awkward and often threatening moments in therapy. This was one way in which professional skills were shared by the trainees, with some additional input from the leader. Recognizing that they could proffer suggestions useful to others was confidence-boosting for the group, and the exercise provided us all with a chance to stock up on useful interventions to employ where contextually appropriate.

Confidentiality

Since the small-group module took place on a course on which I was a member of staff, the issue of boundaries was paramount, given that I was a supervisor, a tutor, a trainer, and the module leader. The issue of "the wearing of many hats" was discussed earlier in this chapter. Where group leaders have also been members of staff of the training institution, there have had to be very clear statements about boundaries between the course components and how issues of confidentiality would be managed. It was agreed between staff members, group leaders, and trainees that the content of the module meetings would not be shared with other course staff. On the rare occasion where an issue arose that I felt should be fed back to the course convenors, I discussed it beforehand either with the whole group or with a particular person if it seemed to be an individual issue. Perhaps naively I thought that on the whole this worked well, although it would appear from the trainees' feedback (Chapter 8) that some anxiety remained about whether their participation in the module would affect their overall achievement on the course, despite my explanations that the module was not an assessed component of the training. Although my efforts to maintain discrete boundaries between these different roles were acknowledged by most trainees in the large and small groups, nevertheless a few remained uneasy.

An unexpected aspect of maintaining confidentiality was the impact of this on some other staff members. When informally interviewing the staff of Institution B (the small group) prior to writing this book, I was generally met with enthusiasm about the trainee-feedback project and interest about the module, but also with a not unexpected uncertainty about what actually took place! It seemed that out of respect for the principle of confidentiality in groupwork, my colleagues had decided not to intrude, despite their natural curiosity. One of them also thought that the group leader could become overwhelmed with the amount of personal information made available during the module; however, this was not my experience: the function of leader should not be that of a therapist, who needed to remember everyone's story, but of a facilitator moving from discussion and experiential exercises to linked clinical issues and potential interventions. As I saw it, my job was to create a forum in which it was possible for the participants to take responsibility for making their own personal and professional links. Sometimes I felt my colleagues experienced me as withholding, and there were occasions when I felt I was. Unless there was serious concern, which had been echoed in the group, about the progress or behaviour of a trainee, I did not feel it appropriate to make comments.

Because of the large numbers and peripheral nature of the course staff involved with the large group, my main conversations about that module were with the course co-ordinator and the director of training, and these focused on administrative matters and not on individual trainees. On the whole, the course staff members went along with this; however, some supervisors felt that they should be advised in advance if supervision was to be the focus of a PPD meeting which would have been feasible in the more structured, pre-planned large-group format.

Where trainees expressed concern about specific aspects of their supervisory experience, they were encouraged to bring the matter to the attention of their supervisors and if necessary to the director of training. Undoubtedly, there are areas of overlap and unclear boundaries between some of the work done in the supervision group in sessions with the tutors and in the PPD; given that these all provide support, learning opportunities, and personally challenging contexts, there are bound to be tensions. In this case, I dealt with the matter as follows. The trainees were asked to discuss, in groups of three or four, how they would manage issues of difference with each other or with someone in authority. By linking their attitudes and behaviour with their previous personal and professional experience, they demonstrated shared difficulties and a variety of coping strategies.

It is not clear whether participation in the module could encourage splits between course staff and the module leader or whether the group forum reduces some of the pressure that might otherwise devolve onto other members of staff. In my experience the latter has been the case. One supervisor commented that since the PPD provided an emotional container for trainees, it could free supervisors to concentrate more on their clinical practice. Another described the group forum as an additional personal learning arena for the "intellectually bound".

Large and small groups

It has been my experience that when working with the large groups the role of the group leader has become more didactic and less spontaneous, especially as meetings were infrequent. As a result, these groups have become more structured and participants have expected more in the way of explanations as to why the leaders were introducing particular topics. This is in contrast to the smaller groups, where it was more often the case that issues were raised by the trainees themselves or reflected something happening currently on the course. When working with the large groups, I was often concerned to maintain a vestige of "crowd control" and therefore took more responsibility for structuring the meetings, hoping that this would also prove more productive. Because of the particular course structure, which meant that the large group met infrequently, both the trainees and the group leaders sometimes felt disconnected from previous sessions. In my experience, for trainees in larger groups to feel that their time is well spent does imply a greater need for direction and structure. Despite this, the majority of participants continued to provide a wealth of energy and ingenuity which led to an atmosphere of goodwill and creativity.

In the small groups, which met more frequently (i.e. three times each week), there was more opportunity for "going with the flow" of the group's preoccupations and less need for the group leader to be quite so pivotal. I went into those groups with a basic theme in mind, should it be required, rather than with a specific format as in the larger groups. This theme may have been connected with unfinished business from the previous meeting, or related to the current stage and demands of the course, or to other issues known to be of concern. However, when the group spontaneously introduced its own agenda, I followed that theme. This often related to trainees' personal experiences and has included issues about partnerships, separation, pregnancy, the death of a parent, illness or absence of a staff member, an arranged wedding, or someone known to be failing on the course. It would have been extremely complicated had the last example involved a trainee with whom I had a supervisory role, and this once again highlights the complexity of multiple roles.

LIFE-CYCLE OF THE GROUPS WITHIN THE MODULE

These groups have a discernible life-cycle: over the years, there has been a very clear pattern of early anxiety followed by a period of excitement, then a feeling of being de-skilled. In the early stages, there is usually little if any overt conflict between the trainees, although friction does become more evident as the group members feel safer to disagree with each other. Inevitably, there is a stage of acute anxiety before the first piece of written work has to be handed in, and then, depending on the results, this may be followed by satisfaction in personal success, sometimes coupled with concern and discomfort about others, who are doing less well. Finally, as might be expected, at the end of the course there is a mixture of relief, achievement, a sense of loss, and possibly some disappointment.

Given the demanding academic and clinical requirements of the training courses, with their fixed time scales in which to produce prescribed pieces of work, it is not surprising that the overall patterns of response over the two years expressed by the various cohorts of trainees, during the PPD groups, is so similar.

CHAPTER FOUR

The use of experiential exercises

The use of experiential exercises must be seen in the wider context of the PPD module in which a great deal of time is given over to current group preoccupations, general discussion, and experimentation with learning new techniques arising out of issues that the group members raise. So the exercises I describe here and in the next three chapters are suggested as possible choices rather than as a programme to be worked through. Some of them may be familiar to the reader from other workshops or training contexts: I would like to acknowledge that many of the ideas have stemmed from such sources. What is different, perhaps, is the way in which they have been developed and now seem to arise organically in these modules.

The use of exercises is perhaps the most innovative aspect of the PPD module for family therapists and is a powerful means of generating an atmosphere conducive to self-reflexivity. The experiential exercises are pivotal in linking past and present personal experience with current professional dilemmas, and they highlight the helpful and hindering effects that the former might continue to have on current professional practice.

Implicit in this approach is a belief that learning to "speak the unspeakable" is an extremely important experience for the trainees themselves if they are to encourage openness in their clients. In the course of considering their own strengths and vulnerabilities, there are opportunities to acquire a range of techniques to cope with these potential triggers in clinical practice. In addition, many of the exercises—for example, Exercise 6: "Personal shields"—could be used as direct interventions in therapy sessions.

In the more active, interventionist style of leadership used in this PPD module, exercises are used to facilitate the process of group cohesion, as a learning tool, and as an enjoyable and often moving experiential method to connect the past and present, thereby making personal and professional links more apparent. As a model of working, I believe that the exercises also encourage creativity and humour and emphasize the importance of recognizing that extending one's own—and indeed the clients'—perspectives need not always be a lugubrious experience.

Whilst trainees are likely to forget a great deal of what one says, they tend to remember certain exercises and their implicit message. When I meet ex-trainees and we talk about the module, they often recall the exercises that they found particularly powerful. These usually include Exercise 4: "Which therapist would you choose?", Exercise 5: "Coming to the clinic for the first time", and Exercise 8: "Sculpting". I believe that these three exercises are particularly effective precisely because the trainees are required to observe themselves and their clients from an unexpected perspective. By training experientially, there is an implicit message that working at a feeling level is as important and relevant as working at an intellectual level, whether with trainees or clients.

The exercises are examples of those most frequently used, rather than being a comprehensive list. As already indicated, exercises seem to develop naturally from the discussions, and although several will have been developed in previous cohorts, the style of presentation, emphasis, and outcome varies on each occasion that they are used. Creating new exercises in the course of a group is exhilarating; in fact, the more experienced and relaxed one becomes as a leader, the more the ideas seem to emerge quite freely from within the group context. Perhaps this process should be renamed as "Improvisation: a therapeutic and training tool".

When an exercise proves to be less than effective, the group can immediately provide feedback, thereby exerting some "quality control". In the ensuing discussion, the trainees might be asked why they thought the leader had introduced that particular activity or concept at that point, and what internal personal trigger or external group or course pressure might have affected her choice of direction. This kind of situation also provides an opportunity to move from the personal to the professional by asking the members of the group how they would handle a situation in therapy when, as therapists, they suggest or try an approach that the family rejects or thinks unhelpful. A role-play might then be set up to experiment with different responses that the therapist could make.

If the group leader is not too focused on the group context, but is also taking wider systems into account, then even the time of year may trigger issues for discussion on which to base experiential work. As described in Exercise 21: "Family patterns", an obvious example is Christmas as potentially a focus for looking at rituals and individual and family traditions and expectations. By being encouraged to consider these issues from a personal and cultural standpoint, the trainees become more sensitized to possible client preoccupations and expectations at these times also.

The reader may be surprised not to find an exercise on genograms listed here; that is deliberate. As mentioned earlier, I agree with the supervisors' view that these need to be done in the supervision groups, where the trainees' personal material can be directly linked to their clinical work. It was also decided that a learning genogram—a map of the trainees' most significant learning experiences, mentors, and books—would be most usefully done in the context of the Teaching module (another course component) rather than as part of the PPD module.

However, the PPD module is not just focused on group discussions and experiential work: the aim is, above all, to link the personal and professional aspects of the trainee. To confirm the latter, role-plays and other methods are used to help the participants experiment with alternative interventions and specific techniques for use in clinical practice. Consistent with the model, these are not preplanned; they are explored and practised as they arise in the course of group discussions and exercises. So, for example, a discussion in which judgemental statements are made could lead to reflecting on personal experience of being assessed and criticized and then to a focus on reframing or positive connotation, or an inquisitorial style in role-play could lead to working on circular questioning.

On the rare occasions that "homework" was set, it tended to be observational or to continue linking the personal work in the group with the trainees' clinical practice. However, in one group, a "homework" task led unexpectedly to a session on task-setting. The group had been asked to observe small children, whether at home, in the street, while shopping, and so forth. The purpose was to emphasize the trainees' existing awareness of children's behaviour, which I thought they had underestimated. However, there was some confusion due to poor task-setting on my part. As a result, the next meeting was spent focusing on techniques of task-setting, including why, how, when, and who participates in tasks, followed by a number of role-plays explaining this process to a "client family".

* * *

On another occasion, a discussion about difficulties in maintaining a focus in therapy led to a spontaneous group exercise in which the designated therapist was asked to stay, literally, on track and physically cross the room while three or four others attempted—by fair means or foul—to prevent this. The trainees

"Staying on track"

produced a number of different strategies, using argument, physical power, status, ruses, and appeals for help; the therapist learnt to bide her time, listen carefully, and respond respectfully, but eventually, battered but unbowed, she completed her journey.

THE EXERCISES

The exercises are described in terms of their *content*, my *comments* about them, *caveats* where there may be possible difficulties in use, and a postscript which I have called *professional pointers*. The specific application of the exercises will depend on the themes that need to be emphasized, as well as the stage of the group's life, rather than on any fixed format.

The timings for the exercises are only rough guides and should not be taken too literally. The same exercise used with different groups may require more or less time to complete satisfactorily, depending on a number of factors. The most significant of these is the size of the group and ensuring that the pace is not hurried, so that everyone who wishes to do so will have the opportunity to contribute. There are no pat responses to these exercises, and it is important to allow time for the trainees to deal with any emotional impact and to have an opportunity to think about the experience rather than rushing on. Where there is a mutually relaxed atmosphere between group leader and trainees, individuals will often choose to raise an aspect of their past or present personal experience and will want time to pursue this. As in therapy, it is important not to rush the process. Although some unexpectedly personal revelations have been made public during the course of the large group, this is less often the case, whereas it is a common feature in the smaller group.

CHAPTER FIVE

The early stage of group life

Over time, we have learnt that it is most productive if the trainees attend the first meeting of the PPD module during their introductory week on the course—preferably on the first day, as previously indicated. The small groups now meet for a total of nine hours each during that first week in order to create an integrated and mutually supportive trainee group as quickly as possible.

In both the large and the small groups, the leader(s) introduce the module, engage the participants, and aim to create an atmosphere of trust, where confidences will be respected; the leader(s) also disclose relevant personal and professional material to encourage this process and to reduce the gap between group member and leader. Because humour is such a tremendous asset in helping people to relax and learn without loss of face, an early aim is to create an atmosphere of playful seriousness.

Throughout the module, the leader deliberately suggests that trainees work in a variety of combinations: sometimes in pairs, for more intimate disclosure; sometimes as a whole group, in order to disseminate a wider variety of ideas; sometimes in their specific sub-groups, such as the supervision groups, in order to confirm their identity. In the pairing exercises, trainees are encouraged to choose a partner whom they know least well, so that the group becomes more cohesive over time. Balking at taking part in exercises is rare, and I usually respond to such reluctance by considering the expectations that we have that clients divulge their all in therapy, and why we think that it is important, and finally link this with the group's ideas about helping other trainees become more involved.

The first exercise takes place at the first group meeting of the module, after the leaders have introduced themselves.

EXERCISE 1
"THE NAME GAME"

> A. One person in the group starts by announcing his first name; the next person announces his own name plus the name of the person who has just spoken and then repeats his own. As you can imagine, in a large group the anxiety builds up as the number of names to be remembered increases.
>
> B. The leader can help out, comment on, and intentionally create more anxiety by interrupting the longer it goes on, encourage playfulness, and so forth.
>
> C. When everyone has had a turn, the leader will have to decide whether to accept the challenge and be the last one to take part. Will it be more—or less—helpful for her to get it right (assuming she can) so that everyone feels remembered, or to be seen to stumble and need help as others have done?

Timing   20 minutes.

Comment   The repetition helps everyone to make connections between names and faces and encourages a sense of mutual recognition. It is the beginning of a process of group cohesion. As the challenge to remember gets harder, some of those who have already had their turn may become very protective and start to prompt those who are struggling, whilst others appear more competitive. These responses often provide early and useful indicators of the ways in which certain group members respond to group situations. It is the beginning of getting to know the participants.

Caveat   I would recommend the use of this exercise for up to—but not more than—30 people. Remember:

- The larger the group, the more time needs to be allowed to complete the exercise.
- If the group is too large, some people who have already had their turn may get bored.

Professional pointers   The way in which people respond to names unfamiliar to them, especially those from other languages, can become a learning exercise in itself. When the naming game has been completed, the group is encouraged to discuss this issue in terms of their own experiences, coping with persistent mispronunciation, and how in practice they deal with clients who come from other cultures and have names that are hard to recognize and difficult to remember.

EXERCISE 2
"WHAT'S IN A NAME?"

This can best be done in pairs, because it gives each trainee an opportunity to get to know another individual before having to speak in the group.

A. Each person introduces himself to his partner in terms of first and family names, as well as any nickname.

B. They then discuss any feelings or events that they associate with their names.

C. General group discussion.

Timing   Approximately 20 minutes.

Comment Allow more time than you might think necessary, as this exercise tends to generate a lot of comment and disclosure of family attitudes and relationships, as well as patterns over generations. Sometimes it can lead to unexpected associations and attributions ascribed to names (Bennett & Zilbach, 1989).

> To encourage an open and more equal atmosphere, I related my own experience of being called Judith, which I described as implying having to be good, sitting up straight, and being utterly conventional. Failure to obtain my "posture girdle" at school finally convinced me that Judith, despite the exciting biblical association with Holofernes, was clearly not the name for me. Paradoxically, I only felt entitled to use the less formal name Judy when I became professionally established and felt that I had earned the choice.

Caveat It is important to move from the pair back into the whole group so as to build up a process of wider group connections. In small groups, feedback can be shared generally; in larger groups, it can be helpful to split into sub-groups of four for further discussion for a short time, before asking for comments from the whole group. This gives more trainees an opportunity to take an active part in the discussions.

Professional pointers Clarification with clients about how they would like to be addressed is not only a mark of respect but can also produce important information. A discussion of the significance of names and connections between family members who have the same name is an extremely useful way to open up discussion in therapy. It often also provides data about cultural practice—for example, there are those cultures in which you cannot name a child after a family member who is still alive, whereas in others a child may be given the name of a respected or loved living relative.

EXERCISE 3
"WHY CHOOSE TO BE A THERAPIST?
DID YOU JUMP, OR WERE YOU PUSHED?"

After each set of questions, allow time for the pairs to do their talking for 5–10 minutes at each of the indicated pauses.

A. Why do you want to be a therapist—and a family therapist at that?

B. If you do become qualified, what will you have proved and to whom?

(pause)

C. Do you think that being a family therapist is a way of finding out more about yourself and your family, or a way of learning how to avoid finding out more?

(pause)

D. What is your family's view of you training to be a family therapist?

E. Who has been the most/least supportive towards you in this undertaking?

F. How do these opinions affect you?

(pause)

G. Think of one strength gained from your family of origin that you bring to the role of therapist.

H. General group discussion.

Timing   Approximately 45 minutes.

Comment   Useful connections may be drawn between therapists' and clients' reflections on corrective or replicative family scripts.

Caveat   If trainees are feeling anxious, they may give rather glib responses initially; if given adequate time to think about the issues, however, it will be a useful exercise at the start of their course.

Professional pointer   Trainees who focus on pathology or go "looking for trouble" in their clinical work may also lose sight of strengths in their own and their clients' families.

EXERCISE 4
"WHICH THERAPIST WOULD YOU CHOOSE?"

This exercise has proved most effective when used on the first day of the PPD module, i.e. before the group members get to know each other. It works equally well with small and very large groups.

A. Four people are chosen by the leader to come and stand in front of the group without speaking; they are selected on the basis of observable difference, which could be related to their style of presentation, dress, age, race, size, gender, etc.

B. The others in the group—the observers—are asked to consider which one of these people they would choose as a therapist for themselves or their family. Throughout this exercise, the group is reminded not to comment out loud, but just to think about the task.

C. After a few minutes, they are asked to think about why they made their particular choice, but again not to voice this.

D. The four potential therapists are then asked to talk to each other so that the group can listen to them; they are also given permission to move around if they wish.

E. After a few minutes, the group is asked whether they wish to alter their original choice; if they do, they are asked to think about why.

(*At this stage, the four are relieved to return to their seats and gratefully merge with the group.*)

F. The observers are then asked to call out on what basis they made their assessment—e.g. was it related to age, gender, etc.—and they are asked to make general comments rather than refer to a particular individual.

G. In pairs—including the four potential therapists—the group is given 10 minutes to think about whether as individuals their perception of themselves is congruent with their trainee partner's view of the impact that they have made.

Timing   35 minutes.

"Which therapist would you choose?"

Comment   This is a very powerful exercise, pushing participants to acknowledge their own biases and to consider how they in turn may be perceived by others. In my experience, most trainees make their final selection on the basis of their first impressions, although occasionally a few change their original choice when the therapists start talking and may become more animated and mobile. The content as well as the style of their interaction with others can prove either reassuring or a limitation.

Caveats

(a) Clearly, at this early stage in the first meeting of the module, trainees are still very uncertain and anxious about being exposed. If those selected demur, the leader usually makes the point that this is a similar situation to that regularly experienced by our clients, who are constantly required to expose themselves—and their dilemmas—in front of strangers. Some genuine explanation that the leader needs some help, and that it won't last too long, usually does the trick. Making it overt that you are seeking difference may make it easier too.

(b) It may be awkward selecting people on the basis of discernible difference such as race, size, or style of dress, but being "protective" and ignoring difference is poor modelling and is not helpful if the aim is to be more aware of the wide range of clients' views.

(c) It is important to allow adequate discussion time for people to make connections between what they are looking for in a therapist and what they themselves might represent to their clients, and how to deal with any discrepancy!

(d) There may be a temptation to rush the process of the exercise to save the four potential therapists from possible discomfort or embarrassment, but succumbing and galloping on will give a very mixed message about the importance of the exercise.

Professional pointer   Therapists can forget how uncomfortable and "on show" clients can feel through having to expose their difficulties in front of strangers, being videoed, and so forth. It is hard to remain sensitive to the novelty of this experience for the clients, especially when as a therapist you are dealing with families on a daily basis. Hopefully, this exercise brings trainees in touch with some of the discomfort experienced by clients.

The purpose of the exercise is to increase the trainees' awareness of how they may impact on others—and to become more self-aware of how their appearance, age, race, gender and physical presentation may impact on clients.

The exercise could be further developed into a discussion about which differences could be comfortably discussed and how the trainees might deal with their own and their clients' disappointments or prejudices.

EXERCISE 5
"COMING TO THE CLINIC FOR THE FIRST TIME"

This exercise is often considered by trainees to have made the most impact in the first few meetings of the PPD module. The exercise was designed to try to address the issue raised by Flaskas and Perlesz (1996) that since family therapists are not required to have any personal therapy, they may not have experience of the client position.

In the first or second meeting,

A. Four or five group members are asked to role-play (Draper, Gower, Huffington, 1991) members of a family coming for therapy for the first time. They are asked to leave the group and create their own brief history and reason for referral and then to leave the building and return as a "family" to the waiting-room of the actual clinic. Since they have only just started the course, the trainees are as unlikely to know the procedures as new families arriving in the clinic.

B. What they have not been told is that the administrative staff have been forewarned and asked not to be too efficient or helpful—to keep the new "clients" waiting, to "lose" the relevant file, and to have difficulty in locating their therapist.

C. The "family" is kept waiting for 5–10 minutes in what is often a crowded waiting-room, including rather fretful, bored young children.

D. Another of the trainees, the designated "therapist", fetches the family and takes them into the therapy room in a very serious manner—even when the shot-gun family laughs anxiously, the therapist plays it straight.

E. The therapy then begins in earnest in front of the one-way screen, for approximately 5 minutes.

F. The family and therapist are given time to de-role.

G. General group discussion.

Timing   1¼ hours.

Comment   As you can imagine, the experience makes a forceful impact. The purpose of this exercise is to emphasize how anxiety-provoking a visit to an institution can be and how people feel less respected when they are kept waiting and are unaware of what to expect. In practice it is not unusual for therapists to continue with

"Group members as 'family' in waiting-room"

their supervision group or team discussions even though they know that the family has arrived and is waiting. Taking part in this exercise and knowing what it feels like to be ignored and kept waiting may discourage this aspect of disrespectful practice.

What is somewhat surprising is the degree to which the trainees, who are "only" role-playing, nonetheless find this such an incredibly powerful and uncomfortable experience. I have wondered whether this might be because in this situation they are forced to think of themselves as being on the same continuum as clients, rather than being able to hide behind their professional status. However, I remain uncertain as to whether the non–role players found the exercise equally as potent.

Caveats

(a) Be on good terms with your administrative staff, and remember to make them part of the plan and to thank them afterwards.

(b) Encourage the observers in the group to get feedback from the "role-players" first before a more general discussion.

Professional Pointer It is often difficult for trainers to convey adequately the essential message that clients and therapists inhabit a similar emotional continuum; therefore, these early exercises focus on attempting to bridge the artificial dichotomy between "them and us"—that is, the professionals and their clients.

EXERCISE 6
"PERSONAL SHIELDS"

A. Each person is given a large sheet of paper; there is a central pool of coloured pencils to choose from. They are asked to draw a shield, divided into four quarters, with items or symbols representing

   i. their family of origin, in one quarter

   ii. themselves as an individual, in another

   iii. their work situation, in yet another

   iv. a close relationship, in the fourth.

B. They are also asked to provide a motto for their shield.

C. They are told that they will be asked to display their shields at the end and to discuss them as much or as little as they wish.

Timing 1½ hours (45 minutes for the drawing of the shields, and the remainder for setting the task and showing and discussing the shields).

Comment This is a powerful tool for encouraging people to think about themselves in a simple way in which symbols may be more immediate and significant than words. This exercise also demonstrates a technique that can be used equally well with clients. By doing the exercise themselves, the trainees are not only involved in a personal experience, but are also learning a new clinical intervention. As can be seen, the individual has to consider himself in relation to four major perspectives. I personally find this exercise quite a challenge: by specifying these four significant areas, it is difficult to avoid thinking about major aspects of the self. Hopefully, trainees doing this exercise will be encouraged to see their clients

"Personal shield"

subsequently as less unidimensional than they might appear in therapy.

It is helpful to remind participants that, over time, what they might draw on their shields will change, depending on their particular circumstances and mood.

Even in large groups, where there will not be much time for looking at everyone's shield in detail, it is important to acknowledge all their efforts and ask everyone to hold up their drawings, in order to show the variety of drawings and symbols. Some people appear much more secretive than others about their shields and will draw the most obfuscatory symbols, whilst others actively enjoy the process of both drawing and explaining theirs. In small groups all participants are encouraged to show and tell.

One very courteous mature trainee, an established academic from overseas, filled her shield with images of serving others. Her motto read "Always consider others first". Feeling emboldened by the trainee's enthusiasm in the group, I wondered whether this was really the motto she had in mind and so asked the trainee what else she might have written instead, pointing out that she could experiment with being uncensored and free to say anything at all. The trainee looked up and then, with great daring, wrote "Oh, fuck it" on her shield. It brought the house down!

Caveats

(a) Some trainees dash through their drawing, but this should not induce the group leader to rush the process; they often come back to their shields and then get more involved with them, especially when they observe their colleagues continuing to work on theirs. If people respond by saying that they cannot draw, clarify that it is not about art but about what can be communicated in another medium. Designing something totally enigmatic or producing an absolutely minimalist drawing can make a considerable impact on the group and can be constructively linked with professional skills, such as how to deal with a family in therapy who opt not to do a task or do it in a minimal way.

(b) Just as it is important to avoid becoming symmetrical or critical of clients who do not appear to take advantage of their therapist's interventions, the same is true of leaders in relation to trainees.

Professional pointer   As commented above, this is a new technique for exploring the creativity of clients and trainees; one in which non-participation is as informative as activity. This exercise is particularly useful in clinical practice when working systemically with an individual or a couple.

EXERCISE 7
"SHARING THE CAKE"

A. The group is asked to think of their favourite cake, an exercise that in itself unexpectedly raises issues of difference in terms of culture, class, appetite, and plain embarrassment!

B. Then they are asked to consider the number of roles that they have currently, e.g. father, friend, social worker, etc.—and to list these.

C. They are asked to draw a large circle representing a cake and to divide it into sections depicting their various roles and the relative size that each takes up.

D. With a different colour pencil or pen, they are asked to draw over these sections depicting how they might like it to be different.

E. They are then asked to consider what they would need to do to change or maintain things to have it as they wish.

F. Then they are asked: if they were to ask their nearest or dearest to look at their cake of two colours, what might their comments be, and how similar or dissimilar would their views be?

G. Finally, in a general group discussion, the group is encouraged to consider the process of doing the exercise, the impact it has had, and how useful they think it would be in therapy with individuals and couples.

"Sharing the cake"

Timing   Including explanations and discussion, a minimum of 35 minutes is needed. Allow 15–20 minutes to stay with the task itself.

Comment   The idea of symbolizing slices of a cake to depict the amount of space allocated to each of an individual's roles was introduced in 1995 by C. P. Cowan and P. A. Cowan during a workshop presentation on becoming a family.

This is an effective way of reducing complicated issues to a manageable proportion in the context of a group. Initially it seems simple, but it can have a powerful effect, leading to trainees having to consider their own situation, how they have organized their lives, and whether this is what they want.

This is one of those exercises that some people may try to rush through without thinking about the implications; however, by suggesting that those who finish quickly wait while the others complete their cakes, it is possible to establish a more serious atmosphere and provide further time for contemplation.

Caveat   Ensure that there are paper and pens available.

EXERCISE 8
"SCULPTING"

Sculpting (see Duhl et al., 1973) is a three-dimensional representational method of communicating a personal experience; it can make an immediate and powerful emotional impact not only on the sculptor, but also on those taking part in the sculpt and those observing the process. Using this technique in the early meetings quickly leads to mutual sympathy and respect as well as to group cohesiveness. The technique is also used to look at systems such as trainees' agencies and other wider networks.

Consistently over the years, trainees have reported that they have found sculpting to be one of the most effective and moving exercises, one that provides a snapshot, capturing a moment imprinted on the memory. Specific examples of participants' sculpts have not been included here, out of respect for confidentiality.

The technique is taught by the leader describing the purpose and method of sculpting, then modelling the process; finally, trainees take it in turn to guide each other through their sculpts, so that the group leader need not remain so central. Great store is placed on attention to details of closeness and distance between family members, and on specific postures and facial expressions. The whole process unwinds slowly, allowing the sculptor to get in touch emotionally with the experience. As little as possible is said, in order to avoid disturbing the atmosphere; the leader or guide stays near the sculptor to offer support and may touch his arm in encouragement.

Although a great deal of emotion may be raised in these sculpts, they should be dealt with in a supportive way by the group and contained by the group leader, rather than becoming the focus of therapeutic interventions. The aim is to model building on strengths and the widening of perspectives rather than hunting for pathology. Where a person is particularly affected by his sculpt, time is allowed to help the trainee express feelings and then move on to linking the past and present. Hopefully this process is therapeutic, albeit not therapy per se.

Sculpting in the context of the small groups is usually started during the block week at the beginning of the course and completed within the subsequent two meetings.

A. Each trainee is asked in turn to sculpt a significant episode in relation to his family of origin. Generally these are static sculpts, but people sometimes feel they need movement to demonstrate their experience more precisely.

B. The trainee is then asked to demonstrate how, if at all, he would have liked the episode to have been different.

C. After each sculpt, 5 minutes or so is allowed for any comments or questions from the group. As more sculpts are presented, the trainees become less hesitant to participate in this way.

D. In a general group discussion, trainees are asked to think about any possible implications for their clinical practice which arose from their own and other people's sculpts.

Timing   45 minutes per person to include sculpting and discussion for each person, plus a brief break of at least 5 minutes between each one.

Comment   Sculpting serves as an initiation rite, in which each participant offers personal material as a *rite de passage* to becoming a member of the group. Trainees virtually always choose to sculpt a traumatic episode from their past, possibly as a way of making the most of an opportunity to explore and find different meanings in such an episode. They have often remarked on the powerful effect of being in someone else's sculpt and experiencing a situation from the sculptor's viewpoint.

Caveats
   (a) The exercise as presented here can only be used with small groups, since each person needs at least 30 minutes.
   (b) These personal sculpts are often incredibly moving, and intensify an experience, so it is important to be respectful and allow the sculptors adequate time to set them up, with pauses for thought, and to re-experience the feelings associated with them.
   (c) It is essential to ensure that all the trainees will have done their sculpts within as short a period of time as possible. Too long a delay may leave some trainees feeling exposed if they have already sculpted their family, and it can create unnecessary anxiety for those still to do their sculpts.
   (d) In the small group, the intensity of the sculpting experience is such that subsequent sessions can feel like an awkward change down from fourth to second gear. A few trainees have been disappointed at the subsequent lessening of that heightened emotional level and personal focus.

EXERCISE 9
"GROUP DYNAMICS—YOU PUT YOUR RIGHT FOOT IN,
YOU PUT YOUR RIGHT FOOT OUT . . ."

In other instances, sculpting has been used to trouble-shoot—for example, on occasions in the small groups, to find out more about conflicts and alliances within a group.

A. A self-selected trainee arranged all the group members in juxtaposition to himself and each of the others in order to demonstrate his view of the closeness and distance between them.

B. This led to some surprise and remonstration.

C. The sculptor was then asked to sculpt the group as he would like it to be.

D. General group discussion.

Timing   35 minutes.

Comment   It is important to specify that the sculptor was merely presenting his own view, rather than "how it is". If no one is prepared to do this, two people can be asked to place two or three others around them and then ask these two mini-groups to place themselves in juxtaposition to each other. Finally, the remaining trainees are invited to put themselves into the sculpt. It may prove confusing, but it will demonstrate alliances and distance between the participants.

Caveat   Stage C can lead to an idealized harmonious group sculpt, avoiding making any conflicts overt. However, the discussion at the end of the exercise often leads to helpful expressions of difference as trainees describe their preferred, and often different, outcomes.

Professional pointer   This is one example of dealing with the concept of "speaking the unspeakable", which the trainees are encouraged to pursue—either verbally or metaphorically.

As the following example demonstrates, sculpting can also be useful as an unplanned and spontaneous technique:

Two trainees wanted to air their differences in the group; after each had described his view of the disagreement and reached an impasse, a third was asked to help each of them sculpt firstly how the situation had arisen and secondly how it looked currently. The two were then asked to demonstrate in turn how they would like their relationship to look. The remainder of the group encouraged them to demonstrate, with a moving sculpt, the steps that would need to be taken to get into this desired relationship. The original pair were then left to discuss the exercise in private while the remainder of the trainees discussed other splits and alliances in the group.

Professional pointers   Learning to sculpt is a technique that can be directly used with clients and when consulting to networks. It is particularly useful with families in which problems have become intellectualized and stuck.

EXERCISE 10
"THERE'S MORE THAN ONE WAY TO MAKE YOUR POINT"

Because of time limitations, sculpting in large groups must be done in sub-groups rather than by each individual trainee. For example, sculpting was used to demonstrate the prevailing mood within the supervision groups and to activate creativity and humour to deal with participants' anxieties.

Leaders of the large groups always tried to find connections between issues that the group members raised and the planned format; when at times this was not possible, we would adjust to their needs, discussing this shift of focus with them.

On one occasion, the group leaders had planned to consider the different ways in which trainees might introduce new and possibly challenging ideas to their clients; the intention was to link this to the ways in which they themselves had learned to cope with change in their own family of origin. However, following our usual opening question—"How are things—what's happening?"—we sensed an extremely high level of anxiety in the group. We discussed this openly in front of the trainees and agreed to change tack. We decided to use the situation to try to normalize some of the participants' worries, to encourage them to learn from each other, and to explore different and creative ways with which they, in turn, could help their clients deal with fears. The emphasis had shifted, from a direct focus on the intro-

duction of change, to how to ventilate anxiety about feeling de-
skilled on a demanding, challenging course.

A. Each supervision group was asked to demonstrate how they
were currently feeling, without relying on the spoken word but
using any medium or resources they had to hand.

B. In order to carry out the task, they first had to share ideas and
feelings between themselves and then devise a communication summarizing these for the group as a whole.

Timing   Approximately 1 hour, depending on the number of
supervision groups: at least 15 minutes is needed for initial discussion and preparation of the presentations, and 5 minutes for
each to be presented.

Comment   The result was both hilarious and inventive. One group
mimed being airline passengers in flight without a pilot, but with a
rather uncertain, tentative stewardess attempting to be in control
as the plane took off for what turned out to be a very bumpy journey indeed. The relief when they landed was almost palpable.
Another used clipboards and pens to devise a colourful board
game based on snakes and ladders, with players making darts
ahead only to be apparently arbitrarily shunted back to the starting
line. Another group precariously balanced various up-ended tables
and chairs into a pyramid, with the four members of the supervision group scrambling—and alternatively pushing, shoving,
and even occasionally supporting each other—to get to the top. Yet
another group was desperately trying to row their boat down the
stream, as one trainee kept threatening their survival by rocking
the boat and finally falling out. The others resisted the temptation
to leave him in the water, and slowly hauled him aboard—he was
last seen waving, not drowning! In a graphic demonstration of
parallel training and domestic pressures, one trainee was first
seen being circled by his three colleagues, each indicating that he
should be doing something different, and then was seen returning
home where his wife and two children each started pulling him in
different directions.

Professional pointer   Whilst metaphor is well established as an integral part of clinical practice, the use of play to make your point is less so. I believe that too often the therapist sets the tone of interviews by her own serious demeanour, which may not take into account the family's natural style, spontaneity, and imagination, all of which could be used in problem-solving.

* * *

Exercises like these were successfully used to encourage group cohesion, to share personal information, and to encourage the use of humour and creativity to dispel some anxieties.

CHAPTER SIX

The middle stage
of group life

The early, intense stage of the module often induces a powerful emotional atmosphere, particularly in small groups.
This can be difficult to maintain in the middle stage because
of the irregularity and infrequency of the module meetings. Many
trainees have expressed disappointment when this loss of momen-
tum occurred. It is essential, therefore, for the group leader to continue to make overt the connections between the personal and
professional persona of a therapist, and to emphasize the inevitable
reflexive loops between the two.

In contrast to the early stage, the middle stage tends to be more
varied in content and therefore in the use of exercises. While the
first five exercises in the early stage were used on a fairly regular
basis in all the groups, the subsequent choice of exercises was less
predictable owing to the different ways in which each group developed. Typically, however, one topic that is always included in the
middle stage is working with children.

EXERCISE 11
"A TRIP DOWN MEMORY LANE"

This is an example of a relatively simple exercise derived from a far more complex source, in this case from the Adult Attachment Interview (Main, Kaplan, & Cassidy, 1985). The aim of the exercise is to encourage the group to get in touch with their early memories of childhood and to extend their thinking to include their wider familial and social systems.

A. The group leader asks the group to close their eyes and think of their very earliest childhood memory and how old they had been then.

B. Next, they are asked:
   i.   to think of two adjectives that would describe their feelings at that time
   ii. to think of who else was present and how that person/those people had responded
   iii. to think of whether this response was helpful or not—and, if not, what they would have preferred.

C. After a 3–4 minute pause for thought, the group is encouraged to call out the ages, the adjectives that they had chosen, and what they thought would have been helpful. These are immediately written on the board by the group leader, to demonstrate the range of ages and feelings that had been invoked, as well as the knowledge that they already had about children's needs for appropriate adult responses.

D. This is followed by a general discussion about talking to children in therapy and about the trainees' specific interests and concerns.

E. At least 30 minutes should be allowed to follow this experiential exercise and discussion with simultaneous sub-group role-plays in which a "therapist", at least one "parent", and two "children" talk together, initially about everyday matters and then about a painful or difficult issue.

F. Allow sufficient time—perhaps 10 minutes—for feedback from the "children" as well as from the "parent". This should be couched in terms of "I liked it when . . ." rather than criticism of the "therapist's" style.

Timing   Depending on the size of the group, 30–40 minutes plus final discussion time and time for role-plays.

Comment   The intention is to stimulate these personal journeys and to combine them with knowledge of children's developmental stages, so as to improve the participants' professional communication with and understanding of the child and adolescent in context.

In exercises such as this, the style of the leader changes in order to move to a more emotional or affective level and to create an atmosphere more conducive to personal exploration. Thus her voice becomes quieter so that the group has to concentrate to hear, her tone is gentler, and the pace much slower, introducing a quasi-hypnotic note, which is reinforced by simple phrases, few words, and repetition.

Caveats
   (a) Working in this way requires a slower pace to allow people time to move from a thinking mode to an experiential mode; briefly glancing around occasionally is sufficient to confirm whether the group is involved in the task. Eye contact should be avoided as this intrudes on the participants' thoughts about the past and pulls them back to the current context.

   (b) Some people get in touch with quite strong feelings during such exercises; it is therefore important to allow time for them to readjust, rather than rushing on.

   (c) It is not always helpful to intervene promptly if someone seems distressed, as they might be making important new connections and may need an opportunity to think about them. However, if a trainee remains unable to concentrate, a quiet word to check if he is all right, or to suggest that he could discuss the issue alone with you or together with the group, as he prefers, is usually enough.

Professional pointer   This exercise clearly demonstrates the four stages of work in the modules—that is, group preoccupation, personal experience, the effect that this has on the therapist, and finally how this can be utilized in clinical practice. This immediate opportunity to link personal stories with professional practice can make a powerful impact.

EXERCISE 12
"A LA RECHERCHE DU TEMPS PERDU, OR EXPLORING THE FAMILY WITHIN YOU"

A. Trainees are asked to bring a photograph of themselves as children.

B. Working in pairs, they discuss their impressions of the photographs, noting differences in their comments.

C. Then each in turn describes ways in which they think they have not changed.

D. There is then a general group discussion of how such an exercise might be useful when working with clients.

Timing   25 minutes.

Comment   This is a useful way of linking past and present, and recognizing that other people's perceptions of a photograph or how you look currently may be quite different from one's own. It also encourages exploration about whether what the onlooker deduces from observing the person in the photograph reflects accurately the latter's underlying feelings at the time that the picture was taken.

Caveat   This requires advance planning to ensure that participants bring a photograph or a drawing.

Professional pointer   Daniel and Hildebrand (1997) describe using photographs in working with a bereaved family to encourage narratives about the past, which is an example of how the same approach can be used both in training professionals and in clinical practice.

EXERCISE 13
"SIBLING POSITIONS, OR WHO COMES FIRST?"

A. The trainees are asked to form into groups according to their sibling position: only child, first-born, second-born, third-born, fourth-born, etc. Very large groups can be subdivided so that more people have time to speak.

B. They are asked to compare their experiences in these groups.

C. They then feed back into the group forum similarities and differences arising from their sibling positions, taking into account gender and cultural issues.

Timing   30–35 minutes.

Comment   This exercise leads to lively discussions about sibling issues and the perceived advantages and disadvantages of their different positions, as well as to the discovery of similar and different experiences within them.

Caveats

(a) This exercise creates a lot of interest; plenty of time—20 minutes—is required for discussion within the sub-groups before the general feedback.

(b) The impact on individual trainees may be very different depending on whether or not they join a group with several others or are on their own. In the latter case, participants could be asked whether they were content with this situation, or would have liked to be included with others and, if so, in which group.

(c) The fact that people from larger families may have had less time to be heard is often reflected in this exercise; it is useful to remind the group that children have varied experiences as they grow up, and it is not helpful if therapists make generalizations that are usually based on their own inevitably limited experience.

Professional pointer   It would be helpful to connect this personal experience with the training task by asking trainees to think about a specific family that they had seen in therapy and whether, and in what way, they had considered the children in the family "as a lump sum" rather than as individuals at different developmental stages, with different needs and a differing command of language and communication.

Understanding the different developmental stages within the life-cycle is essential. Learning how to be with, talk to, and play with children of different ages requires observational tasks and practice. By not adjusting to the child's level of comprehension and language, and by having inappropriate expectations of them, the therapist's behaviour can undermine and confuse both children and parents.

EXERCISE 14
"DRAWING THE FAMILY THEN AND NOW"

A. The group is asked to draw a picture of their family of origin

   i.   when they themselves were very young

   ii. another when they were teenagers

   iii. another currently.

B. In pairs, they are asked to discuss their drawings and comment on any changes or patterns they notice.

C. This is followed by a general group discussion about the process and content of the exercise.

Timing   40 minutes.

Comment   At one level, this exercise provides a method of tapping into links between the trainees' personal development and stages in their family life-cycle, an intervention that could also be employed in clinical practice. At another, it emphasizes yet again that verbal communication need not be the sole method of enquiry.

The act of drawing engages the group, makes a rapid impact at a feeling level, and is economic in terms of time.

Caveat   Provide lots of *coloured* pencils and large pieces of paper.

EXERCISE 15
"ETHNICITY"

A. The group is divided into pairs and asked to discuss the following questions, allowing at least 5 minutes for each question:

   i. How do you define your ethnicity?

   ii. When did you first become aware of your own racial/cultural identity? What precipitated this awareness?

   iii. What was the message from your family of origin or caretakers about your ethnicity? Did this change over time?

   iv. What were the strengths and constraints inherent in this message, and were they affected by different contexts?

   v. How did your family of origin or caretakers deal with racial and cultural difference? Consider overt and covert messages, and share some examples.

B. Each pair is then asked to join with another and in these foursomes to talk about their experience of discussing racial and cultural difference, racism, and the contexts in which such conversations have been particularly difficult or made easier. [10 minutes]

C. Finally there is a general group discussion about implications for dealing with these issues in clinical practice. [10–15 minutes]

Timing   As indicated above.

Comment   This exercise was introduced to me in 1995 by Charlotte Burck in the course of a workshop on race and culture.

EXERCISE 16
"GENDER"

Each instruction is to be alternated with time for discussion.

A. The trainees are asked to divide into pairs and to discuss their views of gender and what it means to them. In particular:

   i.   to think about their upbringing in relation to gender

   ii. to think of sibling and peer issues

   iii. to discuss whether there was a significant difference between those with or without siblings

   iv. to consider whether they have changed their own views of gender over time and, if so, in what way

   v.   to consider how this might affect them in terms of their professional practice.

B. General group discussion.

C. The exercise continues with a series of role-plays. They form into groups of four; within each group one trainee is asked to act as an observer, another as the therapist, and the remaining two as a couple in therapy. The issue is their discomfort in their extended families. In the first role-play, the couple are two gay men; in the second, they are two lesbian women; and in the final role-play, they are a heterosexual couple. The observer finally comments on content, process, body language, and any differences he has noted in the therapist's approach to the three couples. This is then discussed using feedback from the role-play couple.

Timing   1¼ hours.

Professional pointer   Whilst we may intend to be clear and open, we may be unaware of the subtle ways in which we may demonstrate our biases towards couples of the same or mixed gender. This exercise provides an opportunity for giving and receiving feedback. Burck and Daniel (1995) give excellent examples of further exercises to pursue gender issues.

EXERCISE 17
"MIRROR, MIRROR ON THE WALL"

A. The participants divide into pairs and discuss the following:

   i. a word or brief phrase that a colleague might use to describe them

   ii. a word or phrase their partner, or someone close to them, might choose

   iii. words or phrases that the different members of their immediate family, a neighbour, and their clients might select.

B. They then feed back into the group forum in terms of similarities and differences in how different people would describe them and why.

Timing   35 minutes.

Comment   This exercise serves as a helpful reminder that therapists, like their clients, present different facets of their personality in different contexts and in different moods. It may be that where clinicians have a more integrated sense of self and can bring this into their practice, they are less at risk of focusing on their clients' undesirable behaviour as if that was all there was.

Professional pointer   This is a useful exercise to lead into practising systemic interviewing of the individual. It would also be a useful technique for working with a couple, with each of them writing down their responses to each question and then comparing what they have written.

EXERCISE 18
"SWALLOW THAT"

This exercise has been developed following Bennett and Zilbach (1989), who described using an exercise based on food in their training programme.

A. The trainees are divided into groups of three or four in order to discuss their best and most uncomfortable memory in relation to food:

    i.   in their family of origin

    ii. with their own children, or their current close network.

B. They discuss in pairs what themes emerged and what connections there may be between past and present.

C. There is then a general group discussion of how these associations may help or hinder them in clinical practice, especially when issues of feeding or child management are raised as problematic.

Timing   35 minutes.

Caveat   Trainees often get caught up in personal reminiscences and may need encouragement to move on to the final task of specifically connecting their past experiences with their current clinical practice with families.

Comment   Given the significance that food plays in relationships, exercises on the topic can evoke very quick and powerful responses.

EXERCISE 19
"THE CHOCOLATE BAR"

This exercise was created at a point when everyone was very tired and there seemed to be little spare energy. As the group leader, I was feeling that I had nothing more to offer and that an increasingly large pit was opening up at my feet. I suddenly spotted a chocolate bar which had been left on a chair and decided that that was what I needed—but all too soon I realized that everyone else did too. The dilemma was, who should have it? On the principle of "speaking the unspeakable"—that is, giving voice to thoughts that feel too intense or potentially painful to air—which I often espouse to trainees, I declared my preoccupation and built an exercise around it.

The responses were unexpectedly varied, moving, and entertaining, ranging from a straightforward logical approach from a woman with a bad back who said she ached so much she needed the nourishment, to another who said he had diabetes and his blood-sugar level had fallen dangerously, to another who just stood there holding back the tears with a hand out, to yet another—a large man—who crawled around the floor just like a baby with his thumb in his mouth, desperately crying and trying to reach the unreachable. One woman turned cartwheels, another made up an ode to the virtues of chocolate, one sang a lieder, whilst yet another created a diversion and then snatched the chocolate bar and ran off, only to be brought back by a wrathful group. Finally, a sophisticated philosophical case was made by someone who declared no interest in the chocolate but was prepared to be altruistic, to sacrifice himself and accept it, in order to avoid dissension and conflict among his colleagues. Who won? Well, the leader (who had succumbed to the crying baby) had to give way to popular demand and award the chocolate bar to the lieder singer with the beautiful voice.

A. The chocolate bar was placed on a chair in the middle of the group, which sat in a circle.

B. The dilemma as to who should have it was explained, and each trainee was then invited to make a case as to why he should have it rather than anyone else. The group was given 5 minutes to choose a form of plea-bargaining.

C. Each in turn had 2 minutes to present his case to the rest of the group.

D. A decision was to be made based on the leader's judgement of the group's responses to the various pleas.

Timing   40 minutes for a group of 12.

Comment and professional pointer   This proved to be a most enjoyable and creative exercise, which made the point very clearly that there were many ways to try to get what you want or need, and that simply stating your position is not always the most effective.

Implicit in this, of course, is that clients will also address issues in a variety of ways, some of which will move us emotionally while others persuade us logically, which makes it harder to keep the whole system in mind.

Caveat   This is not suitable for a group of more than 15 because of the time factor and the difficulty of maintaining originality. It is important for the group leader not to take a unilateral decision about choosing the winner, but to accede to the group decision. This is consistent with a therapist not imposing judgements or solutions on families.

CHAPTER SEVEN

The final stage
of group life

In the second year of the courses at both institutions, there has always been a tension between the allocation of time to the PPD module meetings and attending to other demands on the trainees' time. Despite a general commitment to the module, other aspects of the course tend to be prioritized. Trainees and group leaders continue to find this frustrating, emphasizing that it is at these very times—when the trainees are under the greatest pressure—that the PPD module, with its capacity to provide containment, is most needed. Nonetheless, because of the exigencies of time, regular group meetings may be forfeited.

On one occasion, a group was so preoccupied with pre-exam concerns that the leader encouraged a discussion and then created an exercise about the different ways in which people express anxiety and the possible effects of their behaviour both personally and professionally, at these times (see Exercise 20).

Another example of competing pressures is when dissertations are in preparation; it can then be difficult to divert the trainees' attention elsewhere. Quite consistently, the module meeting just before the handing in of draft dissertations has proved very uncomfortable: the group leader becomes the main

63

repository of the group's frustration, anxiety, and any disappointments about their experiences on the course. At these
points, I tend to place more emphasis on relaxing the group pace
and acknowledging that the trainees themselves can act as a
resource and provide support for each other. This also provides
a training link with parallels in family therapy when families
may be particularly distressed and lose sight of their strengths.

EXERCISE 20
"COPING WITH GROUP ANXIETY"

A. Each person in the group is asked to think of an occasion when he
   or she was very young and very anxious.

B. They are asked to think about how they had felt and how they had
   responded to the situation.

C. They are asked to recall whether anyone else was involved; if so,
   to consider how the other person or people had responded and
   whether this had helped or hindered them in coping with the
   situation.

D. They are then asked to recall a recent worrying event and how
   they had coped with it. Was it a similar or dissimilar process to the
   earlier one above?

E. Finally, they are asked to talk in pairs about how their own
   experiences and responses could affect their clinical practice,
   when either they or their clients are especially anxious or
   preoccupied.

Timing   30 minutes.

Comment   On some occasions this might be followed by role-
plays of anxiety-provoking scenarios that the trainees had been
discussing. The aim would be to look for alternative approaches
the group could suggest to deal with these issues in clinical
practice. Trainees are encouraged to learn that there is no one
response to a clinical situation; rather, there is a range, depending on which model they favour and what seems to be an appropriate "fit" for that particular family.

Caveat   The early part of this exercise can tap into intense feelings, so the leader should be prepared to take longer over it if necessary.

Professional pointer   This exercise may go on to provide a good opportunity for trainees to practice intervening using a range of alternative approaches based on different systemic models. An hour of extra time should be allowed for this.

EXERCISE 21
"FAMILY PATTERNS"

The approach of the Christmas break is a useful trigger-event for looking at different cultural, religious, and family patterns and how they have evolved.

This exercise starts with personal perspectives, then moves to a consideration of social pressures in the wider community and of how clinicians might address these issues in therapy.

A. In pairs, discuss the significance of Christmas in your family—regardless of your culture.

B. Explain the usual way this period was/is dealt with

   i. in your family of origin

   ii. currently

C. Have any changes been made, and if so what triggered them?

D. Consider any underlying issues—e.g. the different ways in which family members may wish to deal with the event, or a recognition that children may be confused by celebrations at school at Christmas time, given their different religious beliefs.

E. General group discussion.

F. Role-play to experiment with different ways of addressing these issues with families from different cultures and at different life-cycle stages.

Timing   45–50 minutes.

Comment   This exercise usually evokes a lot of interest and feeling, often tapping into dilemmas about following traditional family practices or creating one's own. This exercise is equally effective in small or large groups.

Professional pointer   Given that family therapists are currently working with ever more diverse populations, it is essential to help trainees recognize the significance and differing experience of being in a minority or in a majority. Asking for information about other cultures in this context provides opportunities for therapists to demonstrate their interest and a genuine wish to learn from and about their clients' experience.

EXERCISE 22
"ALL CHANGE"

When there are major changes on the MSc course—for example, someone withdrawing from a course, or two supervision groups being merged, or if trainees change to new supervision groups in the second year—trainees often use the PPD group as a forum for exploring such issues. On one occasion following a general discussion, I introduced an adaptation of an exercise I had first seen in a workshop on stepfamilies given by M. Robinson and D. Smith at an Association of Family Therapy conference in 1992. It was used to demonstrate common ambivalent feelings about moving from one context to another.

A. In pairs, the trainees are asked to talk about a process of change that they have experienced.

B. After 5–10 minutes, usually in the middle of intense conversation, the leader interrupts and each pair is asked to combine with another and continue talking.

C. Ten minutes later, one person from each group is asked to move on to another group (in this way, each group loses one member and gains another).

D. The newly formed groups talk for 10 minutes.

E. General group discussion.

Timing   50 minutes.

Comment   The leader encourages a focus on the *process* of the experience and the effect on everyone of changing the member- ship of the groups. Trainees may raise issues of loyalty to past and present groups, their anxiety about having to start all over again, and fears about how long it will be before the next de- mand for change is made. Trainees often demonstrate a high level of irritation, as well as a degree of excitement at the appar- ently arbitrary nature of the changes. They generally report a concomitant lack of control about the whole experience.

Professional pointer   This leads into skills training in relation to working with separating and divorced families, and step- parenting issues. Role-plays are used in which the above issues are addressed, with a trainee as observer monitoring the direct- ness of information given and age-appropriate language used so that all family members understand what is happening. This discussion often leads to an exploration of the differences—real and imagined—between mediation and therapy.

EXERCISE 23
"THIS HOUSE PROPOSES"

One of the precipitating factors that led us to establish the origi- nal PPD module was a recognition of the increasing gap be- tween the life-cycle stage of "book-learned" trainee therapists and their older, "life-learned" clients. This could cause some trainees to feel overwhelmed and anxious, resulting in an unin- tended lack of respect, defensiveness, or symmetricality. The following exercise has been helpful in recognizing and learning to accept that, all too often, we do not know what we do not know. In many cases, the experiences of an older generation and the premises on which it bases its beliefs become out- moded; more than ever, therapists need to take courage and ask the clients for help in order to be sympathetic and to under- stand their attitudes.

A. A formal debate is arranged : "This House proposes that . . ."

B. The subject of the debate is a firmly held view about a major social change within the last few decades—e.g. culturally and generationally challenging issues such as "divorce is the only solution to an unhappy marriage"; "living with someone if you are not married is immoral"; "adolescents should always do as their parents tell them".

C. Four trainees (a proposer and seconder for each side) are encouraged to volunteer and to declare which side of the argument they support.

D. They are then asked to argue in support of the opposite view.

E. General group discussion.

Timing   35 minutes: approximately 5 minutes per speaker and 15 minutes for discussion.

Comment and caveat   This is a lively exercise which people enjoy, but there needs to be adequate discussion afterwards to consider what was learnt—both from the process of the debate as well as from the content—that helped or hindered them in expanding their perspectives.

Professional pointer   The aim here is to help trainees listen constructively to a view to which they may be initially unsympathetic and which, as a result, could lead them to become symmetrical and disrespectful. Arguing from the opposite perspective tends to make it harder to retain a rigid position. Therapists profit from questioning themselves and their assumptions in the same way as they question their clients and their preconceived views.

EXERCISE 24
"NOW AND THEN"

This exercise is useful towards the end of the course, to monitor personal change.

A. Think about the following, individually:

   i. If you have a partner, what comments do you think he or she would make about any changes in you over the past two years, since you have been on the course? If you don't have a partner, imagine what might be said by someone close to you.

  ii. Repeat this process, thinking of another friend or colleague.

 iii. Would either mention any losses or gains for you, and for themselves?

 iv. How do you think you may have changed, and is this congruent with the views expressed above?

  v. What changes would you like to suggest to the course organizers?

B. Now divide into pairs to discuss your thoughts so far.

C. General group discussion about the advantages and disadvantages of change.

D. Consider a specific family you have seen, and in pairs discuss what the family may have gained and lost through changes as a result of their therapy with you.

Timing 45 minutes.

Professional pointer Encourage the trainees to think about specific details of the changes that they mention, thereby stimulating them to be more curious about detail in their clinical practice.

EXERCISE 25
"TAKE YOUR TIME"

There was a period when two or three particular trainees tended to wander in late for module meetings, and this was clearly noticed by other participants. On the first two occasions, I briefly recapped the meeting so far, but on the third occasion I deliberately continued with the discussion without further explanation to the latecomers. They appeared a bit surprised but then began to concentrate in order to catch up.

The issue was later tackled as follows, without making overt links to the trainees' poor time-keeping:

A. The group was asked to think about

   i. what being late signified to them

   ii. how they dealt with their own and other people's lateness.

B. They were then asked to link this with their own upbringing and their family's attitude to lateness.

C. Finally, they were asked to consider how they perceived and dealt with their clients' lateness in clinical practice.

D. General group discussion.

Timing   25 minutes.

Comment   The ensuing discussion may reveal negative comments about clients' "resistance" when late for therapy sessions, in contrast to therapists' rationalizations in relation to their own tardiness.

EXERCISE 26
"PUTTING IT ON PAPER"

As Bacigalupe (1996) comments,

> Writing can play an important role in aiding clients and therapists to include multiple voices and diverse positions in their communications. . . .
>
> There is the potential for therapists as well as clients to see themselves as storied individuals, their lives as an evolving text. [pp. 371–372]

A. The group had been talking about working systemically with an individual, and the mood had become quite introspective. Tapping into this, I suggested that each person made a list of chapter headings for their autobiography, which would highlight salient internal and external events, important influences, special people, life-cycle stages, etc. This activity evoked a great deal of interest and quiet contemplation; it seemed to be a rapid method of bringing the past into the present, observing patterns over time and ideas of continuity.

B. During the general group discussion that followed, the trainees were asked to consider whether they might use this in their clinical practice either during a therapy session or as a set task. The method could be applied to an individual, the story of a couple, or a family's narrative.

Timing   30 minutes.

EXERCISE 27
"THE SNAKE EXERCISE"

This is a popular exercise used to emphasize possible connections between an individual's behaviour in a group situation and in his or her family of origin.

A. The group (the larger the better) is asked to form a ring, holding hands.

B. They are told that they are free to move and do whatever they like, with the one proviso that they must not let go of each other's hands (this symbolizes their connection with their family of origin, regardless of whether it is positive, negative, or exists only in phantasy).

C. They are then encouraged to run, jump, get apparently inextricably intertwined, wrapped round each other, etc. Don't be surprised at how little encouragement is needed to create mayhem! When they look impossibly enmeshed, they are exhorted to try even harder.

D. They are then asked to freeze in their position, however uncomfortable it is, and then to shout out in one or two words how they feel, and to note their position in the group.

E. They are then asked to unravel themselves and return to their original circle—but, of course, without letting go of each other's hands.

F. When they finally manage this, amidst much laughter and acrobatic contortions, they are asked to think about the process that made it possible for them to return to their original circle.

G. Then they are asked to think of one or two words to describe their position in their family of origin.

H. Finally, they are asked to consider if there was any similarity between their position in the group and in their family of origin, and between the words they chose to describe both. For many people, this proves a fruitful exercise, in which they can make unexpected powerful connections—for others, it may just be fun, but as the exercise tends to stay in the mind hopefully the message about the links between the past and the present may too.

Timing   20 minutes.

Comment   This can serve as a useful ending ritual, in which everyone is actively involved, connected to each other, required to collaborate to reach a solution, and enjoying themselves.

Caveat   This exercise requires lots of space and is very energetic!

"The snake exercise"

GENERAL CONSIDERATIONS

1. The pace of groupwork must take into account and respond to the preoccupations and energy levels of the trainees.

2. It is important to allow enough time at each stage of an exercise for emotions to surface and, at the end, in order to process them.

3. Clear connections between the personal experience and the professional application of the concepts should be made.

4. It is essential to allow time for discussion rather than relying on too many different exercises.

5. The larger the group, the longer the time required for feedback.

6. In the large group context, it can be helpful to subdivide the group into smaller working units for some of the time, in order to give more participants an opportunity for active involvement.

7. If gaps in training are spotted (e.g. as in the case of the "homework" task to observe children, in Chapter 4), it is important to weigh up the advantages of tackling these in the group setting as opposed to suggesting that supervisors might deal with specific issues in supervision groups, or informing the course convenors about the omission.

8. There are many important topics that could usefully be included in future modules but for which no exercises have been given here—for example, the impact of illness, disability, ageing, class, and spirituality. The exercises described in these chapters reflect the issues raised by trainees in the cohorts between 1993 and 1995.

CHAPTER EIGHT

Trainee survey
and commentary

Colette Richardson & Frankie Zimmerman

T
his chapter is the result of Judy Hildebrand's wish to include the views of those who had participated in the PPD
module, which prompted her to invite us, as ex-trainees, to
share our experiences. As we felt that our views alone would not be
sufficiently representative, we decided to talk to other trainees in
order to amplify our impressions.

This "talking" took the form of a semi-structured interview, the
questionnaire for which is presented in the Appendix. We would
have preferred to have compared the two groups, from Institution
A and Institution B, at the same point in their training so that we
could simultaneously look at the similarities and differences in the
trainees' experiences; however, as these courses in the two institutions do not run concurrently, this was not possible.

JH made the original contact by letter to all the then current
trainees from Institution A and the ex-trainees from Institution B,
explaining our interest. They were asked to indicate whether or not
they would be willing to meet us in order to share their views.
Twenty current trainees from the large group of thirty-six in Institution A volunteered to take part, compared to all nine ex-trainees
from Institution B. The different response rates could be explained

by the fact that trainees from Institution B had trained with us (between 1993 and 1995) and, perhaps out of a sense of loyalty, felt more "duty-bound" to participate. Furthermore, at the point of interview, our colleagues had, like ourselves, completed their training a year previously and therefore had had an opportunity to integrate their experiences and reflect on the contribution made by particular aspects of their training. In contrast, the trainees from Institution A were, at the time of interview, still heavily involved in research projects and essays and in coping with the resultant pressures.

Seven participants from each institution were selected for interview, chosen on purely pragmatic grounds: firstly on the basis of their speediness of response, and secondly on their accessibility. There was an even spread of male/female participants. We were delighted with their enthusiastic response and enjoyed talking to colleagues who co-operated and shared their views so willingly.

Having completed our conversations, we then had the task of condensing the material into a manageable format. We did this by grouping the feedback into a number of categories that, in our view, represented the main themes that emerged. We wanted to give a "flavour" of the kind of comments that were made and have therefore chosen quotations from the semi-structured interview to highlight the essence of what the trainees said. These themes are presented under two broad headings:

1. Aspects of the module which trainees found useful.

2. Aspects of the module which trainees identified as needing some change.

ASPECTS OF THE MODULE
WHICH TRAINEES FOUND USEFUL

The experience of vulnerability

"Sometimes it was like we were in a position clients might be in. . . . the fact of how tentative and nervous you feel, . . . sensitive to any sort of criticism, makes you realize how clients must feel like that too."

". . . to be asked to look at your own experiences and to be reflecting on them . . . in a context where you don't know people . . . where the power is not entirely yours . . . and being observed."

These quotations give a flavour of how being a participant in a PPD group helped trainees become more aware of their clients' experiences. Feeling vulnerable, powerless, exposed, and de-skilled were helpful in this process. Several features of the PPD module contributed to this increased awareness, including the giving and receiving of feedback within the group, being on the receiving end of exercises such as role-plays and sculpts, and being in the "learning position". Trainees identified this "window" into the experience of being a client as playing an important part in developing their clinical practice. They also recognized the similarities and differences between their experience as trainees starting a new course and client families arriving at the clinic for the first time. Exercise 5, in which trainees role-play a family arriving at an institution and being met by administrative staff, was identified as particularly effective in addressing "new beginnings".

The provision of support

"I quite like reflecting on things with the group, so I think the times when we talked, particularly when things were difficult . . . it was an opportunity to say what you were actually thinking and find out whether other people were thinking the same, and then you felt part of the group—and I think that is very supportive."

". . . a forum for getting together with all these people that were on the course with you and doing something that wasn't about listening to a lecture. You did exercises with them and you learned things about them. . . . It provided you with a sense of belonging to the group and to the course. . . . It made you feel . . . 'these people are like me'."

Specific to trainees from Institution B was the supportive and sustaining role of the PPD module. These trainees really valued being able to discuss and share their experience as a whole. It was important for them to know that they were not alone in managing the demands of their training. This was especially relevant at times of anxiety generated by deadlines for assessed coursework. This need for support was heightened at times of change both within the staff group and within the training group, as, for example, when other trainees left or were asked to leave the course.

An intensive first week

"It was a real intensive backdrop to . . . facilitate the getting to know each other in a very stark and intimate way."

The first week of the training course in Institution B was considered highly significant. This was an intensive period when trainees participated in the PPD module for a total of nine hours spread over three days of that week. During this time, they used each other to represent family members and sculpted a significant experience from their own family life. This was mentioned by everyone as an important and memorable time, setting the tone and creating a cohesive and supportive group.

Although not seen as supportive per se in Institution A, the PPD module provided a meeting point which, in itself, created a sense of "belonging" both to the group and to the institution.

The opportunity for self-reflection

"I had to confront the way I present myself as a victim, and what it really helped me to challenge was making an active choice, throwing myself into things more, being committed to processes that I'm engaged in . . . being more assertive rather than saying 'poor me'."

"Role-play is about trying to be empathic with families' systems, putting yourself in someone else's shoes, and in doing that you actually learn something about how they feel but you also learn something about yourself."

". . . It's the continuous awareness of power, the power of those family relationships . . . as a template for how you function in the world."

The trainees are referring to the module as providing an opportunity for them to become "observers" to themselves and hence the possibility to challenge their personal, family, and professional scripts. They were challenged to think about their assumptions, including what is "normal," their personal style (e.g. the use of humour), how they presented themselves in professional relationships, and to become aware of aspects of themselves that had previously been underplayed.

From our conversations, the trainees valued those exercises that had assisted them to become more aware of their own assumptions, as, for example, when asked to consider a range of questions regarding gender, race, and culture (e.g. Exercises 15 and 16). At the beginning of each course, the group leaders in the two institutions invited trainees to participate in an exercise called "Which therapist would you choose?" (Exercise 4). This gave the trainees an opportunity to realize the importance of first impressions and to become aware of the impact that they might have on clients. Others exercises that they mentioned were the adapted Adult Attachment Interview, "A trip down memory lane" (Exercise 11), which seemed effective in reawakening powerful memories, and "Personal shield" (Exercise 6), which encouraged trainees to depict different aspects of themselves in relation to their family of origin, their intimate relationships, their work setting, and their sense of self. The latter exercise led in subsequent discussions to identifying issues common to their own and their clients' families; one shared example was a history of the experience of migration. Our impression was that the exercise encouraged trainees to compare and reflect on how their own family experiences were both similar to and different from those of other trainees.

Learning through action and fun

"What was most helpful were the exercises around getting out of your head . . . role-play exercises where we described the group physically [sculpting]. It was as if the link between what you think and what you feel is made at the same time, so it's like reading and hearing something together. It makes it stand out . . . it is a more powerful experience than just being told or talking."

"We all had to compete for some chocolate. . . . It was fun. It was a bit like taking a risk . . . self-revealing . . . you couldn't just be professional . . . there was humour."

Trainees frequently referred to the "experiential" emphasis of the module, particularly their pleasure in participating in exercises that required action rather than words—for example, one in which they were asked to convey non-verbally the effects of the course on their significant relationships. This allowed trainees an opportunity to be creative and demonstrate aspects of themselves that are less frequently called upon. The effect of this was to increase their confidence, and it led some of them to expand their professional style and clinical repertoire. Trainees appreciated this experiential aspect of the group leaders' style, which they said provided a contrast to the necessarily verbal emphasis of the rest of the course.

Personal revelations

"It was supportive . . . the group leaders talking about their own professional development."

Trainees particularly valued the times when the group leader(s) shared experiences from their own family and professional life. In doing so the leaders were perceived as "human", and this encouraged trainees to share their own "stories". It was also important for trainees to discover that the leaders were experienced in the field and could draw on a breadth of expertise, which included using different therapeutic models. This helped to validate those trainees who had brought with them training experiences other than family therapy.

The group leaders' understanding of course demands

"In theory it would have been better to have someone external. However, I don't think that that would have been practically useful and would miss out on the richness of someone who knew . . . the stresses and strains of the course."

This quote sums up the dilemma that most of the trainees expressed regarding the position of the group leader, although they
believed that having a group leader external to the course would
offer clearer boundaries between the PPD module and the rest of
the assessed aspects of the course. However, having an internal
group leader meant that the role was filled by someone with intimate knowledge of the demands of the training. On balance, trainees valued the group leaders' internal position and knowledge of
the stresses, strains and rhythms of the course.

* * *

The above comments highlight aspects of the module that were
considered useful by the trainees from both institutions. There
were some variations between institutions in that trainees from
Institution B additionally found the following to be useful.

A co-created agenda

"I liked spontaneity—the fact that it wasn't pre-planned, that the
group leader built on where the group was at."

Trainees appreciated the fact that the module was not pre-
planned, as in this way their current preoccupations could be taken
into account; this in turn gave them a sense of being co-creators of
the agenda in each session.

The broadening of clinical repertoires

". . . being more reflective and able to change the intensity of what
happens in the session."

While recognizing that the MSc course as a whole had helped to
broaden the trainees' range of therapeutic skills, some felt that the
PPD module had made a particularly important contribution in
this area. The trainees indicated several ways in which their skills
had developed—for example, they reported increased confidence
in using humour and playfulness with families, more awareness of

the positive aspects of their clients' lives, more ability to respond to feedback in the room and to change the emotional tone or direction of the therapy. They also felt more willing to use anecdotes from their own experiences where appropriate and generally to feel less self-conscious. We wondered if these changes had come about through the trainees' participation in exercises that lifted them out of their usual style or mode of interacting. Having experienced themselves differently in the context of the module, were they then able to experiment with an increased range of behaviours in the clinical context?

ASPECTS OF THE MODULE WHICH TRAINEES IDENTIFIED AS NEEDING SOME CHANGE

Size of the group/safety

"I came with a prejudice about the size of the group and my prejudice was confirmed. The large group was too large to feel safe, and I only spoke spasmodically and usually to people on a one-to-one basis."

Trainees identified aspects that needed changing in order to promote greater safety, in particular the size of the large group and its infrequent meetings, which left the trainees feeling inhibited, unable to share personal information, and reluctant to engage with the "process" of the module. Whilst they appreciated the fact that many of the exercises took place in sub-groups, the fact that the membership of these varied inhibited the development of trust.

Another aspect that they raised as requiring change was in relation to the group leaders' role/roles on the course. For trainees from Institution B, the issue of safety was associated with the multiple roles held by the group leader, because JH was the personal tutor or clinical supervisor to several trainees. This combination of roles almost certainly contributed to some of the trainees' worries about confidentiality. (This reflects JH's concerns regarding multiple roles, as outlined in Chapter 3.) Although they had been informed that the PPD module was not an assessed component of the course, nonetheless they were still worried that information could be shared and might affect how they would ultimately be assessed.

They suggested that the group leader's role in the assessment and evaluation process could be more emphatically clarified from the outset.

Opportunities for raising dissatisfactions with the rest of the training course

"I would want to say something about the evaluation process by the group about the group. . . . I was wary and therefore kept quiet when at times it might have been pertinent to speak."

"It might have been helpful to deal with things earlier on . . . which is, what role or venue is there for us as trainees to take up grievances or problems, without us feeling inhibited from doing that because we are being assessed?"

The majority of trainees expressed the desire for a context in which they could express any dissatisfactions and grievances with the training course. While it was recognized that the PPD module could have a role in meeting this need, clarity and reassurance pertaining to confidentiality were named as factors needing further institutional consideration. One suggestion was that an external consultant mediate between the trainee and course staff if difficulties arose in these relationships. The problem appeared to be that trainees feared that by using the existing mechanisms for dealing with disagreements with course staff, they could put their course assessment in jeopardy.

Insufficient attention to diversity

"The course was very good at looking at gender perspectives but less good at looking at race."

"1 think that having two group leaders is important because it is one way of bringing diversity, but from the gay perspective, having (two heterosexual) group leaders, this is not diversity."

Trainees felt that opportunities within the module had been lost for developing their thinking and for exploring ideas in relation to diversity, such as disability, homosexuality, and ethnicity. This left some trainees feeling isolated and perhaps further marginalized, whilst some felt burdened by the task of having to raise trainees' awareness themselves.

The lack of integration

"I think that at times it felt as if the module wasn't closely linked to what was happening—for example, within supervision groups and issues that people were trying to grapple with in their work and training."

Trainees were critical of the MSc course in terms of lack of attention paid to the impact of the training on their work contexts. They would have appreciated help with the struggle that they experienced integrating and applying their new-found learning. A further area of integration identified as being absent was that more acknowledgement and attention should have been given in assisting those trainees who experienced difficulties trying to incorporate their previous therapeutic model(s) with systemic ideas. This was summed up by one trainee who "felt like a jack of all trades and mistress of none".

They would also have welcomed greater integration between the different components of the training and the PPD module. For example, trainees would have liked a stronger connection between the content of the academic seminars and that of the PPD module. Without this, they felt that the possibility of using the module to explore related ideas and practice new skills was undermined.

"It was important to have a space where you could explore different issues but I could have got more out of it had it been more connected to the academic seminars."

Trainees in Institution A added that the following aspects needed further attention.

Fixed agenda

"It felt that they obviously planned it beforehand and it didn't actually take note of what else was happening on the course."

As a result of the greaters numbers in the large group, the content of the module was, in the main, pre-planned. The effect of this was that they had less influence over the agenda, and consequently their current preoccupations were not always addressed.

SUMMARY

In obtaining the information presented in this chapter, we had two questions in mind:

1. Is the PPD module considered useful by trainees, and, if so, why?

2. What could be changed to make it more useful?

We hope that our findings will not only be relevant to the further development of the module in these two institutions, but will also be of interest to other trainers responsible for designing systemic and possibly other training courses.

We acknowledge that the way we have interpreted the feedback is also a reflection of our own assumptions and experiences and is therefore biased in terms of the questions we have asked and the way in which we have chosen to make sense of the material. What emerged is as much to do with our own beliefs as it is to do with those who were involved.

Overall, the PPD module was thought to be a useful and worthwhile component of training by everyone interviewed. It provided a supportive forum where trainees could explore some of their own experiences and any effects that these may have had on their role as clinicians. Generally, the feedback gathered from Institution B was more positive than that from Institution A. In the latter, trainees expressed dissatisfaction with the structure of the large group, which in turn made it more difficult for the module's potential to be realized.

In understanding the differences in the feedback from the two institutions, it is important to note that the course members from Institution B have remained in contact since the completion of their training, meeting for peer supervision on a regular basis. As "insiders" of this group, we had our own assumptions as to what our colleagues were trying to voice in their conversations with us. In contrast, our knowledge of the trainees from Institution A was limited to contact during the interviews. It could be argued that trainees from Institution B might have felt the need to view their experiences within the module more favourably in order for the group to remain connected. The other side of this coin could indicate that these favourable experiences, such as the supportive relationships that developed within the module, prompted the group to continue contact post-training. It is also possible that these trainees felt constrained by their current relationship with the interviewers and therefore less able to share uncomplimentary stories of the group experience. Equally, the trainees from Institution A might have felt freer to talk about their dissatisfactions because of their distance from the interviewers.

The trainees did not express a common view about the purpose of the module. Some saw it as a setting for reflecting on their life experiences and their possible effects on the business of working with clients, whereas for others it provided a context for the development of clinical skills. Some trainees wondered whether or not it was an attempt to provide an alternative to personal therapy whilst others felt that the provision of a PPD module fudges the question of whether systemic therapists should have their own therapy. These views reflect the current debate within the field and the different discourses within the training organizations as to the necessary components for training effective systemic therapists. In the view of those whom we interviewed, the PPD module, despite its identified shortcomings, is a useful and valuable component of a systemic training regardless of whether or not personal therapy becomes a requirement of family therapy training.

CHAPTER 9

Reflections

In this final chapter I connect the trainees' feedback with some of my original speculations, before moving on to comment on a number of related training issues for the future.

On the whole, the message from those trainees who took part in the survey confirmed many of the earlier reasons for setting up the module. For example, they concluded that taking part in experiential work had helped them to become more sensitized to their clients' experience of therapy; they appreciated the variety of ways in which they had been encouraged to reflect more carefully on what it felt like to be in their clients' shoes.This could be described as a development of their capacity to use empathy and compassion in their professional role.

They also commented on the significance of the leaders' role in helping them to bridge the gaps between their own and their clients' experience, between their personal and professional persona, and between their theoretical knowledge and their clinical practice. They also demonstrated the proposition that "Optimally, the self and the role of the therapist can exist in an acknowledged, functional, creative and respectful marriage" (Haber, 1994). The trainees confirmed my belief that if the leaders shared some of their own experiences with the group, this could lead to group members being more open; it would also become self-evident that the need for maintaining confidentiality was a mutual one.

As anticipated the group experience per se was acknowledged as a potentially beneficial forum for learning, provided that factors of size, frequency, and regularity of meetings could be ensured. The nine hours allotted to the PPD meetings of the small groups (Institution B) during the first week of the training proved invaluable, rapidly creating a cohesiveness within the groups. Further positive effects commented on by group leaders, course staff, and trainees include the trainees' willingness to work together, a sense of mutual support, and a considerable degree of openness. What is less clear is whether there would be a shift in the ethos of the module from a personal/professional training tool towards a more therapy-oriented milieu if the groups were to meet more frequently. Some recognized parallels with clients voicing their feelings and opinions "publicly" in the process of therapy. A common denominator between families in the early stages of therapy and trainees in the early stages of training is that everyone is vulnerable to feeling de-skilled, despite their competence in other aspects of their lives.

One unexpected outcome was the rapid establishment of personal connections between many of the trainees in the small group within the first few intense meetings of the module. This in turn appeared to produce a more relaxed effect in the supervision groups as well as a greater openness between the staff and the trainees. However, due to the size of the large group, trainees complained of a lack of safety in the group and, as a result, felt uncertain about how much to invest in it. Thus we may have missed an opportunity to support the emotional needs of some of these trainees during the course of their training and their changing epistemology. Typically, many would be dealing with major personal events during the two years; for example, in a recent cohort of thirteen, six trainees or their partners became pregnant. Others have had to cope with major losses, such as bereavement and separation, changing family structures, conflicting personal and professional demands for time and energy, moving house, changing jobs, and so forth. In addition, many described their social life as being put "on hold". One trainee summed up the experience of being on the course by quoting her sister, who said: "After two years, I'm glad to have you back." In some cases, in response to some of these stresses, trainees have opted for personal therapy and hence to the potential model confusion described in Chapter 2.

Trainees may have a variety of motivations for being on the course: for some, it may be predominantly a question of career advancement; for others, it may have more to do with curiosity and a wish to develop new ideas; for yet others, there may be an element of wanting a break from the routine of their jobs. An early supposition was that regardless of the circumstances, the PPD module might have a role in helping trainees to recognize their adventurousness in taking on new challenges and learning the inevitable limitations of what any training course—or, indeed, family therapy itself—could offer. A useful parallel could be drawn here with the clients' experience and expectations of therapy.

The module was used as a "safe-enough" setting in which to air complaints and grievances. The large groups may have been more prone to use the group context to seek out support for their views from trainees with whom they rarely had contact. They also might have felt freer to do so, because the group leader(s) at that time were external to the course and therefore not involved in their assessment. As discussed in Chapter 3, participants in the small groups may sometimes have been more inhibited because I was both the module leader and filled other roles on the course.

My original hope, confirmed by the trainees' responses, was that the module would help trainees to acquire a greater awareness of the complexity of becoming a therapist through the lengthy discussions, the use of experiential exercises, and the skills training across systemic models. My assumption was that an expansion of their repertoire of responses and techniques could lead to therapists being more flexible and therefore more likely to find a suitable "fit" with their clients. Clearly, research is needed to validate these impressions.

LOOKING AHEAD

During the time it has taken to produce this book there has been an upsurge of interest in trainees' personal training needs in Europe; no doubt this has been spurred on in Britain by the establishment of the United Kingdom Council for Psychotherapy (UKCP). As a result of this move to a greater coherence amongst psychotherapists, some differences in training methods in the various family therapy teaching institutions have now become more apparent. This may have spurred on the recent encouraging move by Confetti—a group of representatives of the various family therapy institutes—to hold discussions about possible approaches to the personal and professional aspects of family therapy training.

In my view, the particular PPD module described here is one such valuable training approach. In the past, there has been some confusion as to the purpose of this PPD module—that is, whether it was intended to be a form of therapy or a form of skills training. I believe that this confusion partly reflected an uncertainty and lack of concensus as to whether work on the self of the therapist was a training requirement. The lack of an over-arching policy in the field remains a controversial issue, but as trainers in family therapy we do have the responsibility for declaring our position. It is true that some trainees may not feel the need for self-exploration in a therapeutic context; however, I would argue, as stated previously, that having such an experience can induce greater empathy with clients, and that it is likely to lead to therapists' greater self-reflexivity and thus may avoid inappropriate attributions.

> The therapist's personal family life has both immediate and remote determinants and, if unexamined, can play a major (though unconscious) role in shaping the therapist's ideas about fairness, normalcy, and the appropriateness of roles in family life. The therapist cannot escape his/her background but may be able to use it advantageously in building certain kinds of alliances. It is imperative that therapists be aware of the nature of their personal family experiences and the influence these experiences exert upon them. [Catherall & Pinsof, 1987, p. 157]

An opportunity for personal exploration both in therapy *and* in the PPD module is, in my opinion, more likely to produce therapists who are more competent and more compassionate.

Although I believe that ideally trainees should have personal experience of family therapy, there is a case for spreading the net wider. For those trainees unable to attend with their families/partners for a few (two to four) family therapy sessions, I would propose that inviting significant others outside the immediate family network could be a viable alternative. For example, some trainees have commented that they had already worked on family issues, and their current preoccupations tended to be related to their work situation; this group might find it more relevant to invite professional colleagues instead. Another and possibly more feasible option might be to invite trainees to attend with member(s) of their friendship network, given that the latter might now play a more significant role.

The difficulties of drawing in geographically distant, possibly unmotivated, and otherwise-occupied family members, friends, or colleagues should not be minimized. But I am not convinced that these difficulties are insuperable if, as trainers, we are prepared to experiment with a variety of options. If we can agree in principle to the need for some experience of personal therapy for the trainees, then we will also need to tackle the following questions:

1. Should there be consistency in the model of therapy?

2. Should the context of therapy be within or external to the course?

3. Should therapy take place prior to or during the training?

4. How many sessions are required?

5. Who will provide the therapy, and how will it be paid for?

6. Should the training institutes establish a roster of accredited family therapists to take on this presumably short-term task?

7. Should trainees be required to report on the experience, and, if so, in what form?

8. What safeguards for confidentiality will be required?

From the point of view of equal opportunities, we would have to ensure that selection for a place on the course would not favour those who chose *family* therapy, rather than any other option, for personal exploration.

Equal opportunities

If family therapists reach consensus in favour of personal therapy as a condition of training, this could lead to only those who can afford private therapy being eligible for training. Courses are already extremely expensive, professional bodies are providing less financial support, and a further outlay could preclude some trainees from less well paid sectors such as social work, nursing, occupational therapy, and teaching from applying. Indirectly, this could affect the number of people from minority cultures coming into the field, since a large proportion enter through these routes. Given that the availability of therapy on the National Health Service is already extremely limited, the likelihood of making more such time available for training purposes is extremely unlikely. Will this lead to yet another situation where unto those who have (the means), it (the opportunity for therapy) shall be given?

Equal opportunities for acceptance on courses may also unwittingly be eroded if, at the point of selection, when all other criteria are matched, preference is given to trainees who have already had some personal therapy. If it is the case that previous therapy is seen as a positive weighting factor, trainers could reasonably be accused of being disingenuous in not declaring this as a precondition or an advantage in terms of selection for training. Any such statement would also have to clarify which model, if any, would be prioritized.

Without research to suggest otherwise, then common wisdom, the therapist's own knowledge, and an accumulation of clinical experience have convinced many therapists that personal therapy, which leads to greater self-reflexivity, does make an appreciable difference to competence in therapeutic practice. If this is the case, what are the implications for those therapists who did not have such an opportunity? Would they have had a more equitable chance to become more competent and sensitive if personal therapy had been made mandatory?

To take it a step further, could it be said to have been unethical not to provide training in a mode that was consistent with the trainers' own beliefs, reflected their own experience, and was considered by them to be in the clients' best interests?

Ethical issues

In emphasizing the interaction and overlap between personal and professional dimensions, there is a tacit assumption that trainers have the right—and indeed the responsibility—to intervene in relation to private issues where these, in the trainers' view, impinge either on the trainees' clinical practice or on their capacity to manage the demands of a rigorous training. Would it not also be ethical for all training institutions to make a formal statement to this effect?

Deciding on the nature of personal preparation required on a family therapy training is a complex issue. To be both logical and consistent, the trainee treating families should have the experience of being in therapy with his own family. However, even if trainers were convinced that it was a necessary process, and trainees were willing to issue the invitations, what right do we have to make such a powerful intervention in these family systems—what pressures are we indirectly exerting on behalf of one member of a family who chooses to pursue a particular career? In any case, it is unlikely that all family members conscripted in this way would be willing or feel the need to expose themselves in therapy. Pursuing such a policy could create a further dilemma in relation to equal opportunities: would those trainees whose family or partner was unwilling to undertake therapy not be eligible for selection on the course?

In an effort to deal with this apparently contradictory situation, many trainers are already recommending systemically based individual therapy rather than individual psychodynamically oriented therapy for family therapy trainees, in the hope that this will prove to be more consistent with our theoretical model. However, this does not disguise the fact that being a client/patient in any form of individual therapy is a very different experience from the immediacy and complex interactions of being in couple or family therapy.

Over time, trainees have commented on their confusion arising out of differences in theoretical models and the contrast between their experience of individual therapy, whether systemic or otherwise, and their clinical practice with families. This was not just

about being a therapist in one situation compared to being a client/
patient in the other: it seemed to have more to do with differences
in technique and belief systems. This, in turn, raises the issue of
the desirability of congruence between the therapist's personal experience of therapy and the systemic therapy that they practice, a
logical as well as an ethical conundrum that could have serious
implications for training. As trainees have said, straddling two
models is not just uncomfortable: more importantly, each model is
likely to invalidate the other, and this could ultimately undermine
both personal therapy and professional training.

Enthusiasm and over-optimism can sometimes lead trainees to
have unrealistic expectations about their clients' pace of and potential for change during the process of therapy; there is a similar risk
of assuming that any form of personal therapy will somehow also
be able to transform the person of the therapist. Since no form of
psychotherapy can produce a panacea, a more realistic goal would
be an increase in the trainee's self-reflexivity which in turn would
lead to an increased perception of the complexity of the process of
change in oneself and others. Hopefully, an increased curiosity
about oneself, as explored in therapy, generalizes to a healthy and
productive curiosity about others.

It is important to acknowledge that within the different institutes here and abroad, trainers are experimenting with a variety of
different approaches to the personal/professional issue. Examples
include trainees making videos of their family and bringing them
in to training for discussion; others are invited to take up some
exploratory family therapy sessions with their family or partner at
the start of the course; Hildebrand and Speed (1993) recommend
"at least one lengthy consultation with each trainee and close
friend, partner or family not to look for problems but to give them a
first-hand experience of the way in which such encounters affect
people" (p. 337). Some institutions use a traditional groupwork approach to focus on personal issues, while others argue that a close-
knit family therapy team, working behind the screen, acts as a
safeguard, noting therapists' trigger-points and often commenting
on personal and professional links. Selvini-Palazzoli (Selvini &
Selvini-Palazzoli, 1991) has described teamwork as a personal resource for the therapist. At the Prudence Skynner Family Therapy

Clinic in London, a focus is maintained on the trainee's genogram, which is introduced as early as the pre-course selection interview and continues to be worked on throughout the training. Another position is that adopted by Hedges and Lang (1993), who employ "mapping" as a major method.

How systemic are we?

Moving away from current training methods, I would like to address the possibility of taking on a more innovative, proactive role in seeking out other systemic opportunities within training. I believe that many of us have paid insufficient attention to the people who will be most immediately affected by the trainee's preoccupation during their training. It could be both informative and reassuring for family members, a close friend or partner, or a professional colleague to meet the staff, to have an opportunity to ask questions, and to be told about the stages in the training that are likely to be particularly demanding. An informal event with staff and trainees, and the latters' choice of "significant other(s)" might also give the trainees an opportunity to demonstrate their competence and maturity in a role other than that of trainee.

Whatever decision is made regarding the integration of personal and professional aspects of training, I feel that there is also a need for a more informal contact between our trainees, those tangentially affected by their training, and ourselves.

There seems to me to be insufficient commitment, whether at a social or information-giving level, to reduce some of the mystique and anxiety surrounding "The Course". I have a suspicion that time limitations are not the only reason this does not take place; it is as if trainers have found it more comfortable to be *teaching about* family and wider systems than to be *systemically interacting* with them. The avoidance of such contact to date seems to me to reflect a psychoanalytic-theory base rather than being consistent with a systemic perspective.

THE FUTURE

In this book I have described one way to "mind the gap" between personal therapy and professional development using a module that focuses on the links between trainees' past and current life experience, their professional development, and clinical skills training in the group forum. In terms of improving the model, there is still more work to be done in relation to balancing and blending discussion, experiential work, and specific skills training as well as addressing the issues raised by the trainees. The inclusion of this or a similar module will hopefully be a serious consideration on training courses, although it may be less popular in contexts where senior trainers may not themselves have been trained in personal exploration. Where trainers are sympathetic to these ideas, they may have to compete with pressures of academic requirements and the perennial issue of time allocation. Has the time come for personal/professional development of family therapists to move from a position of marginalization to one of prioritization? I concur with Mason (1997) that "unless family therapy can make significant changes in relation to this issue—the exploration of 'self' in therapy and thus in training—the respect given to it as a psychotherapy will ultimately diminish".

APPENDIX

Trainee survey questionnaire

We are two graduates from an advanced family therapy training programme, and we are interested in the effects of the Personal and Professional Development Module on therapists.

In order for us to understand the relationship between the PPD module
and clinical practice, we would like to ask you some questions to explore this further and thank you for participating in this project.

Your confidentiality is assured. Names and any identifying material
will be changed.

1. Sex of trainee (M/F)

2. Age range:
   21–30 years
   31–40
   41–50
   51–60

3. Basic professional training, including any family therapy training prior to this most recent advanced training course.

4. Type and length of course undertaken/being undertaking.

5. What is your idea of the aim of a PPD module?

6. Does/did this module fit with your expectations? Please describe.

7. Please pick out examples of any experiences during the course that were significant to you and explain why.

8. Did they affect you personally? If so, in what way(s)?

9. Did they affect you professionally? If so, in what way(s)?

10. Do you think that you have changed as a therapist during the course? If so, in what ways (e.g. being more creative)?

11. Could you identify in what ways, if any, the PPD module has contributed to bringing about these changes?

12. Of all the different PPD module exercises/experiences, which have you found the most helpful/significant?

13. Please describe one or more such examples and explain why you found them to be significant.

14. One of the purposes of a PPD module is to increase self-reflection in the therapist. Has this been your experience? If yes, what made this more/less possible? What helped/hindered this process?

15. What impact has this had on your work (i.e. the ability to be self-reflexive)?

16. Do you think your experiences in the PPD module have made you more sensitive to the emotional experiences of being a client?

17. If so, how was this achieved?

18. If this was not your experience, please explain.

19. How do you think this module fits in with the rest of the course?

20. What effect did this module have on your relationship with the rest of the course? For example, did it help you to manage the other demands of the course?

21. Has it helped sustain you throughout the course?

22. If *you* were running this module, what would you keep the same and what would you change or add?

23. Did/do you have any other course connections with the leader(s) of the PPD module (e.g. as your tutor, supervisor)? If yes, what impact did/does this have?

24. Given that some trainees did/do have other connections with the group leaders(s), what impact did/does this have on your experiences in the PPD module?

25. What relationship do you consider the PPD leader(s) should have with the rest of the course? Would it have been more/less useful if the PPD leader had been external to the institution?

26. Would you agree that there is a link between your own experience in the PPD module and a family's experience of therapy? If yes/no, can you amplify?

For Institution B trainees only

27. How helpful has it been having two group leaders?

28. How important has it been to have had a male and a female group leader?

For all trainees

29. Were/are there any issues that you feel should be/have been addressed in the PPD module?

30. Did you make any fresh connections between your personal life and possible effects on your practice?

31. Can you name and identify specific skills that you acquired from the PPD module?

32. Overall, do you think that the PPD module is a worthwhile use of time?

REFERENCES

Aponte, H. (1994). How personal can training get? *Journal of Marital and Family Therapy, 20* (1): 3–15

Aponte, H., & Winter, J. E. (1992). Training the person of the therapist in structural family therapy. *Journal of Marital and Family Therapy, 18*: 269–281.

Bacigalupe, G. (1996). Writing in therapy: a participatory approach. *Journal of Family Therapy, 18* (4): 361–373.

Bennett, M. I., & Zilbach, J. J. (1989). An experiential family therapy training seminar. *Journal of Psychotherapy and the Family, 5* (3–4): 145–157.

Blow, A., & Piercy, F. P. (1997). Teaching personal agency in family therapy training programs. *Journal of Systemic Therapies, 16* (3): 274–283.

Boscolo, L., & Bertrando, P. (1996). *Systemic Therapy with Individuals*. London: Karnac Books.

Bowen, M. (1978). *Family Therapy in Clinical Practice*. New York: Jason Aronson.

Burck, C. (1995). Developments in family therapy in the last five years. *ACPP Review & Newsletter, 17* (5): 247–254.

Burck, C., & Daniel, G. (1995). *Gender and Family Therapy*. London: Karnac Books.

Burck, C, Hildebrand, J., & Mann, J. (1996). Groupwork with separated and divorced women. *Journal of Family Therapy, 18*: 163–182.

Catherall, D. R., & Pinsof, W. M. (1983). The impact of the therapist's personal family life on the ability to establish viable therapeutic alliances in family and marital therapy. *Journal of Psychotherapy and the Family, 3* (2): 135–160.

Cecchin, G., Lane, G., & Ray, W. A. (1994). *The Cybernetics of Prejudice in the Practice of Psychotherapy*. London: Karnac Books.

Cooklin, A. (1994). Response to Haber. *Journal of Family Therapy, 16* (3): 285–291.

Daniel, G., & Hildebrand, J. (1997). *Families & Loss* (teaching video and booklet). London: Institute of Family Therapy.

Draper, R., Gower, M., & Huffington, C. (1991). *Teaching Family Therapy*. London: Karnac Books.

Duhl, F. J., Kantor, D., & Duhl, B. S. (1973). Learning space and action in family therapy: a primer of sculpture. In D. A. Bloch (Ed.), *Techniques of Family Psychotherapy—A Primer*. New York: Grune & Stratton.

Flaskas, C., & Perlesz, A. (1996). *The Therapeutic Relationship in Systemic Therapy*. London: Karnac Books.

Francis, M. (1988). The skeleton in the cupboard: experiential genogram work for family therapy trainees. *Journal of Family Therapy, 10*: 135–152.

Haber, R. (1990). From handicap to handy capable: training systemic therapists in use of self. *Family Process, 29*: 375–384.

Haber, R. (1994). Response-ability: therapist's I and role. *Journal of Family Therapy, 16*: 269–291.

Haley, J. (1996). *Learning and Teaching Therapy*. New York: Guilford Press.

Hardy, K. V., & Laszloffy, T. A. (1995). The cultural genogram: key to training culturally competent family therapists. *Journal of Marital and Family Therapy, 21* (3): 227–237.

Hedges, F., & Lang, S. (1993). Mapping personal and professional stories. *Human Systems, 4*: 277–298.

Heinl, P. (1987). The interactional sculpt: examples from a training seminar. *Journal of Family Therapy, 9* (3): 281–291.

Hildebrand, J., & Speed, B. (1993). The influence of therapists' personal experience on their work with couples. In: J. van Lawick & M. Sanders (Eds.), *Family, Gender & Beyond* (pp. 331–338). Heemstede: LS Books.

Lindsey, C. (1993). Family systems reconstructed in the mind of the systemic therapist. *Human Systems, 4*: 299–310.

Main, M., Kaplan, N., & Cassidy, J. (1985). Security in infancy, childhood, and adulthood: a move to the level of representation. In: I. Bretherton & E. Waters (Eds.), *Growing Points of Attachment Theory and Research* (Monographs of the Society of Research in Child Development, Vol. 50, Serial no. 209, Nos.1–2). Chicago, IL: University of Chicago Press.

Mason, B. (1997). *The Exploration of Self (Personal Development) in the Training of Family and Systemic Psychotherapists*. Discussion paper, Confetti London meeting.

McDaniel, S. H., & Landau-Stanton, J. (1991). Both and . . . Family of origin work and family skills training. *Family Process, 30* (4): 459–471.

Onnis, L. (1997). *Synoptic Table about Training Programs: General Criteria in Different European Countries*. Private publication (EFTA board member).

Real, T. (1990). The therapeutic use of self in constructionist/systemic therapy. *Family Process, 29*: 255–272.

Selvini, M., & Selvini-Palazzoli, M. (1991). Team consultation: an indispensable tool for the progress of knowledge. Ways of fostering and promoting its creative potential. *Journal of Family Therapy, 13*: 31–52.

Street, E., & Rivett, M. (1996). Stress and coping in the practice of family therapy: a British survey. *Journal of Family Therapy, 18* (3): 317.

Whitaker, C. A., & Bumberry, M. (1988). *Dancing with the Family—A Symbolic-Experiential Approach*. New York: Bruner/Mazel.

INDEX